❀

The Art of
James Thurber

The Art of James Thurber

Richard C. Tobias

OHIO UNIVERSITY PRESS
Athens, Ohio

8175
T536T

To Emily

Preface

This book was conceived at 10:00 in the morning on the 26th of September, 1961. I had just come back to my office from a morning class and found there a friend with an idea. He had noticed that although American publishers issue innumerable studies of major American writers, no one pays attention to "the good, second-rate writers." He wanted to remedy this lack with a series of "interim" pamphlets reporting on good but critically unnoticed contemporary writers such as James Thurber.

I winced to hear him include Thurber in the category of "good, second-rate writers," but I did not know—since I am not a specialist in American literature—that ten scholarly essays appear on Faulkner or Hemingway to one on Thurber. I grew up reading Thurber, and I assumed that in the reckoning of scholars, Thurber would rank where he ranks in my understanding: equal to his celebrated contemporaries although different in method. A year earlier, I had begun to teach a course on comedy. I teach the course backwards, that is, I start my classes by assigning contemporary comic writers while I explain basic methods of comedy and then move backwards to try out the methods in examining the comedy of Twain, Pope, Molière, Shakespeare, and Aristophanes. Thurber seemed a natural and right place to begin. When I chose him, I thought of him neither as first-rate or second-rate; I chose him simply because I knew he would appeal to my students and because he seemed a worthy member of the company of recognized writers of comedy. I was amused, and not amused, that my friend should think of Thurber as second-rate, and immediately I began to plan how I could convey my amusement to Thurber when I wrote to tell him that I wanted to undertake such a study. A telephone call from my wife interrupted our conversation; she wanted me to take her to our maternity hospital immediately. While she was in the labor room, we talked about the project. In the week that followed my youngest daughter's birth, I had no time to write to Thurber or even to think how I could tell him the funny story without upending the skittery Thurber temper. Just eight days later, on the 4th of October, 1961, he suffered a blood clot on the brain while speaking to the cast on the opening night of Noel Coward's *Sail Away* at the Cort Theater. We followed the news closely as he rallied, as he underwent surgery, and then caught pneumonia and died on the 4th of November, 1961. Thus what was to have been an interim report on a living writer now became an attempt to assess Thurber's claim as an artist.

In assessing him I have been fortunate in receiving the support and help of many people. The Charles E. Merrill Foundation made available to the University of Pittsburgh a number of Faculty Fellowships in the Humanities, and during a summer free from teaching made possible by one of these fellowships, I wrote the first draft of this study. The award was granted through the office of Dr. Charles Peake. A number of friends have read various drafts of the manuscript and offered help and advice. If what they read here differs greatly from what they read before, the improvement is due to their kind attention and encouragement. Fred Hetzel, Ralph Allen, Emily Irvine, Nancy Dean, Nathalie Allen, Clark LaMendola, Charles Crow, Suzanna Downie, James Marino, Mercedes Monjian, Alan Markman, Donald Tritschler, Alun Davies, Robert Marshall, and all my students have contributed. They looked at me and expected me to be clear and convincing.

I would like to thank Simon and Schuster for permission to quote from Clifton Fadiman, editor, *I Believe* (New York, 1939) and Harper and Row for permission to quote from E. B. White, *Second Tree From the Corner* (New York, 1956).

Mrs. James Thurber kindy read the manuscript, annotated it, queried it, and argued fiercely with me about it. Fannia Weingartner, my editor, has read with taste and intelligence, and she often has made my meaning more clear even to me. My wife has been loving and tireless, and the book should be dedicated to her, but it is dedicated instead to Emily Tobias since on her birthday the book was conceived. The gestation was longer and the labor pains (it seems to me) much more protracted.

Richard C. Tobias

Contents

The Art of
James Thurber

Introduction

A writer of comic material succeeds or fails on the simple question of whether he is funny. Immediately after the visceral laugh, however, a good reader may ask why he laughs. Keats starts a sonnet with the question:

> Why did I laugh to-night? No voice will tell:
> No God, no Demon of severe response,
> Deigns to reply from Heaven or from Hell.
> Then to my human heart I turn at once.

Keats asks, in effect, how can we laugh in the terrible world that we know. Writers like Keats do not laugh, and when they turn to the human heart they seem to go to a world more important than the world of laughter. I want to understand the technique of the art the comic writer practices. My aim seems a simple aim, but realizing it is very difficult. Although grand pronouncements on the social value of the comic writer's reports or the moral value of his attacks on human foibles would be easier, I want to judge comedy as an art form. It will be apparent that Northrop Frye and Susanne K. Langer help me to find a language to study and admire what is in the comedy of James Thurber. I have also consulted other critics (see Additional Reading List, p. 186), for although few critics write about comic writers, a host have developed theories of comedy, frequently invoking Gods and Demons. Since Thurber gave us his world and said we were welcome to it,

I have tried—with the aid of these theorists—to see what Thurber's comic world is.

I have also used Robert Morsberger's *James Thurber* (Twayne's United States Authors Series, no. 62, 1964). The book is valuable for its careful and full "Selected Bibliography" which includes a thorough listing of Thurber stories and sketches not reprinted in his books. Morsberger's book is also valuable as a first attempt to explain Thurber and to relate his comedy to the events of the twentieth century, but Morsberger says very little about Thurber's first book, *Is Sex Necessary?* and comparatively little about his five fairy tales, *The Thurber Album,* and *The Years with Ross.* His major concern is the essays, stories, and sketches, and he has a fine chapter on Thurber's drawings. Further, he prints all the biographical facts (the facts are common currency) and relates Thurber's life to Wolcott Gibbs, E. B. White, Mark Van Doren, Elliott Nugent, Dorothy Parker, Robert Benchley and others. Gibbs, White, and Nugent, of course, contributed to Thurber's art when they edited him and collaborated with him. Thurber met Hemingway, Faulkner, and Fitzgerald when they came to New York, and, although neither Morsberger nor I can point to dates and titles, Thurber surely read them well. In expanding Walter Blair's pioneering *Horse Sense in American Humor* and the few other critics who have had the temerity to pass judgment on Thurber, Morsberger helps to place Thurber in the American tradition. Without in the slightest taking away from Morsberger's achievement, I must also be grateful to him for making me know better what I had known before—that Thurber needs careful study and admiration.

I see no point in duplicating Morsberger's excellent work on bibliography, biography, the drawings or Thurber's general themes. I do not write about the Thurber who is a biographical fact but about the Thurber who exists in his comedies and sketches. He is a comic fiction who is a representative American figure. The Thurber I write about is the man who ventures into the world of our common experience and brings to it the skill of a rigorous comic craft. The comic-fiction Thurber changes the facts of his life, even distorts them (recall what Aristophanes does with Socrates), for the sake of his comedy. The world of his books deserves primary attention. I pay a great deal of attention to *Is Sex*

Necessary? even though it is neither his greatest work nor his most characteristic and is a collaboration with White. I re-examine some of Thurber's early sketches in order to find Thurber's comic patterns. A new analysis of *The Male Animal* is necessary because the play signals a change in Thurber's comic methods. I am very much interested in his fables, his tales, and in his last books on his friends in Columbus and his friend Harold Ross.

I write the biography of a sophisticated craft. Although Thurber's themes are often repeated, the craft in presenting them develops and changes. What prompted the different stages of the development is difficult to know, but I can suggest some reasons. The persistent influence of Henry James is evident and acknowledged, as is Thurber's self-proclaimed debt to Benchley, E. B. White, Ross, and others in the *New Yorker* and Algonquin crowd. From them and possibly from his Ohio soil, Thurber acquired all the lineaments of the romantic impulse, but in the sea-change to his world the impulse gets considerably jostled. Romantics, like Keats, are rarely funny; when their subjects and aims enter the world of comedy, Thurber has profundity tempered by comedy.

In a Preface, "My Fifty Years with James Thurber" (*The Thurber Carnival*), Thurber writes that "In his prose pieces he [Thurber] appears always to have started from the beginning and to have reached the end by way of the middle. It is impossible to read any of the stories from the last line to the first without experiencing a definite sensation of going backward." Therefore I begin at the beginning to show that his subjects in his first book are the common coin of twentieth-century American experience. Secondly I show how *My Life and Hard Times* and other books of the thirties use social and literary types. His exploitation of conventions marks him as a superior comic artist. *Let Your Mind Alone*, *The Male Animal*, and a sequence of drawings, *The Last Flower*, show how Thurber uses the ancient comic plot and discovers a new variation on it. In *My World and Welcome to It* and *The Beast in Me* he finds new ways in which the comic characters are attacked by the flux of human experience. Using his Fables, I show how the comic principle of continuation (keep on doing a thing and an audience will laugh) establishes comic values and, at the same time, universal truths. In his Fables the clash between the seemingly antiquated fable form and his contemporary meaning makes rich comedy. Thurber's five tales of strange and marvelous adventures, written at the end of and after the war, illustrate how a comic writer contrasts the appearances of our world with fantasy; *The White Deer* is the best known of these tales. In the Fables and the tales, Thurber works his way from the familiar wasted landscape into a new vision. Finally in *The Years with Ross, The Thurber Album*, and his last collections of sketches and essays Thurber tests his comic insights by once more looking at social attitudes and conventions that every American knows.

I have chosen sketches which illustrate his developing comic craft; I did not want to bore my reader by extended descriptions of all his sketches, and I want the reader to take pleasure in discovering pieces that I don't discuss. I have limited myself almost completely to work published in his books. A great many Thurber sketches are still lying in the files of the *New Yorker* and other magazines (Morsberger lists them), but I am content to remain in his published collections since he chose those for me.

I

The Pleasure Dome

In 1929, a thirty-four year old ex-middlewesterner, ex-news-paperman, failed novelist, parodist, and managing ediior named James Thurber published a book in collaboration with his friend E. B. White. The book is called *Is Sex Necessary?* and it sold 40,000 copies. From then until his death in 1961, James Thurber published twenty-five more books of sketches, essays, stories, made thousands of drawings, collaborated on a play, and appeared in a revue based on his own writing. His work should be called a pleasure dome of the American imagination. The books have all been read; they enjoyed success and earned Thurber livelihood and honor. His name appears in newspapers; suburban dogs are named for him and for his affection for the creatures; a physician has described a Walter Mitty syndrome in imitation of Thurber's most successful fictional character. His books continue in print. Although there is mention of his name and his work as a kind of social phenomenon, no one has assessed his contribution to the American imagination. To be sure, Robert E. Morsberger has written *James Thurber* (Twayne's United States Authors Series, no. 62, 1964), but Morsberger's excellent book is a starting place — collecting information and sorting out themes — rather than a sustained examination of Thurber as an artist. A new study has been announced. Robert Elias' essay in *The American Scholar* is excellent, but there is no sustained study of all of Thurber. It seems strange that a nation which is eager to praise its own genius has not praised Thurber more, but possibly our ignoring his work merely follows the familiar habit of slighting our genuine man of talent, like Poe and Melville, until a foreigner discovers him. I do not think we should wait for a foreigner to find Thurber for us.

Thurber trampled all over Walter Blair's *Horse Sense in American Humor* in an essay called "Memoirs of a Drudge" and all over Otto Friedrich in "The Tyranny of Trivia" because Friedrich had "recently stumbled upon the body of my work lying sprawled and unburied on the plain, and was distressed to discover that it had been ravaged by trivia." In an essay Thurber wrote for Clifton Fadiman's anthology *I Believe* Thurber objects to the meddling intellect of the critic. Such prohibitions against criticism are, while threatening, answerable. Another prohibition, that we lack a means of evaluating comedy, is fear-inspiring but need not be stultifying. A final reason, the lack of biography, is not at all persuasive since we have his books, the proper subject of study and pleasure.

The twenty-five books, one play, and one revue provide God's plenty and the pleasure dome which they construct in our imagination is finished, ready for our praise and understanding. His work, to make discussion easier, falls into three natural periods. In a creative period that runs from 1929 to 1961 his work falls into three clusters, one for each decade. The first group, starting with his collaboration *Is Sex Necessary?* and ending around 1937, develops the comedy of the little man menaced by civilization. In addition to *Is Sex Necessary?* Thurber published his comic autobiography *My Life and Hard Times* and three other collections. These essays and sketches, originally written for the *New Yorker*, are witty excursions into the impossibility of life or heroism because of large women, automobiles, and the flummery of a complicated civilization. Peter De Vries says that in these books Thurber puts into action a comic Prufrock, an epithet which is both appropriate and accurate. The characters never quite dare, and when they do, they are squelched by dogs, psychologists, women, shower faucets and overcoats. These books contain the vintage Thurber; he springs to life full-grown in them without any faltering juvenalia. At thirty-four, when the first book was published, he had behind him a long career on newspapers and in literary tasks to train him in mastery of the English sentence. The first question

Ross asked him when he started to work for the *New Yorker* in 1927 was "Do you know English?" He knew what he was doing then and very quickly Dorothy Parker and Baird Leonard knew he was a writer and not the managing editor that Ross tried to make him. Thus, not surprisingly, when we speak of Thurber men and women, Thurber dogs, and Thurber situations, we think about these earliest sketches. All the essentials are there. He started with a unique character and style but only few of his critics realize that his style and character develop and mature.

The *Last Flower* (1939), a cartoon sequence with a minimum of prose commentary, and *Fables for Our Time* (1940) inaugurate a second phase of his writing. He refurbishes old themes, probes more deeply into human experience, and tries new methods: in this period he collaborates on a play, discovers the fable form, and writes his children's books. In January, 1940, his play *The Male Animal* (written with Elliott Nugent) opened for a successful run in New York; for the first time the tart, astringent Thurber dialogue gets a larger framework. His three collections of essays may appear to continue the old habits, but the laughter in them is muted and the stories advance toward a terror that the earlier stories suggested but did not explore. But the most important work in this decade, I am convinced, is to be found in the fairy tales. These stories appear without warning—except as the fables themselves have announced a different direction—but in them he advances his insight and his art. His five tales are the only books that were written to appear without prior magazine publication. Thurber makes no particular claim for these five books (he mentions them only once and then slightingly when he talks about his work), but they seem to me to contain the quintessence of his vision. Although the stories seem to be written for children, they are more rich for an adult mind that catches and enjoys the outrageous tricks played in them upon experience and time. Like *Alice in Wonderland*, each book is larger than its words seem to indicate. The books of the 1930's show him as an amusing and effective critic of manners and behavior, but these tales show him an interested and acute critic with subjects echoing up and down our own and the general American experience. He works his way through the comic despair of the 1930's to an imaginative reconstruction of experience that explains and comments on that experience. To know Thurber is to know these books, and it is a measure of the unsatisfactory and slight criticism that he has received that no one (with the exception of Edmund Wilson in a review of *The White Deer*) has had the courage to explore their meaning.

Thurber never abandons his old methods, but he is always developing new ones. Thus he continues to write sketches, fables, and children's stories in the 1950's, but he also discovers a new way to communicate the vision he has learned in the books for children. In *The Thurber Album* (1952) he returns to the same autobiographical subjects he exploits in his third book, *My Life and Hard Times*, but he returns to them with the benefit of the insight dramatized in the children's stories. He considers once more the remembered time of late nineteenth- and early twentieth-century America. He pits his remembrance of the past against the fact of mid-century and, in the contrast, the reader intuits, senses, a third possibility that neither accepts all of the past nor rejects all of the present. Thus we discover a golden vision beyond the remembered past and the sad present. *The Years with Ross* (1959) is similar; it looks back to a heroic time to contrast that past with a disturbing present and to envision a New Found Land. He now writes a comedy of fulfillment; his heroes and heroines are menaced by civilization, as are the heroes of the tales, but they find a way to surmount its obstinate mindlessness, carelessness, and disrespect for intelligence. They live against all odds. The characters act against a debilitated landscape; when they touch a thing, however, "the ugliness, God knows how, goes out of it." And he is convincing.

The writing of the 1930's creates a kind of *Inferno*, the writing of the 1940's a *Purgatorio*, and the writing of the 1950's a *Paradiso*. Of course, the inferno is frenetically gay; the purgatory contains a vision; and the paradise is tinged with so much regret that only the astute reader catches its vision. Further, it is audacious to suggest that a twentieth-century writer has Vision; to describe him that way is a nasty way of condemning him. Visions of paradise are not common, and when tried, they seldom satisfy. The fact remains that these last books do satisfy, and I am astonished that no one yet has shown why. Thurber continued to write his sketches, fables, and stories, and in the most effective of these pieces his anger and his vision (both always potential) are rigidly and thoroughly dressed in what has become a perfected artistic form. He waits now for readers able to see the value in these last examples of his art. The purpose of this examination of Thurber's comedy is to give his readers the necessary techniques to know how well Thurber triumphs in submitting his wide American experience to the style (the grammar, I would like to say) of the comic vision.

If Thurber's writing has sufficient development and subject matter to attract our attention, two large "No Entrance" signs are posted outside his work to warn us off again. Thurber himself posts one; our attitude posts the second. Any critic of Thurber is going to walk softly because of the treatment critics, both real and fictional, receive in his comedy. Thurber's own sign is spelled out in his response to Otto Friedrich's essay, "James Thurber: A Critical Study" in a paperback annual, *Discovery* (No. 5, 1955). Friedrich praises Thurber highly, and, among other things explains Thurber's interest in and use of Henry James, the important influence of E. B. White, and the connection between Thurber, and James Joyce and T. S. Eliot. Any lover of Thurber will learn much from Friedrich's placement of Thurber in the American tradition, but Friedrich makes the great mistake of saying that Thurber's "sketches fulfill a constant need for money, and probably also a need to write about trivia." The testy, Thurber temper snapped back not on the canard about money, but on the question of trivia (see p. 14). Great artists make solemn asses of their critics and Thurber succeeds on Friedrich in "The Tyranny of Trivia" just as he succeeds earlier in comments on Walter Blair, Marxists, Freudians, and academic critics. He never praises a critic (though Mark Van Doren says that he had a weakness for English professors) and a series of sketches in his own notebooks, letters, and biography pretty well succeed in reducing the critical act to absolute trivia. The story "A Final Note on Chanda Bell" *(Thurber Country)* brilliantly mocks the whole enterprise of criticism. In the story the narrator, a literary critic, is driven to distraction for fear that his painstaking analysis of Miss Bell's abstruse (and maybe obtuse) fiction will stand "as a monument to fatuous gullibility." I watch constantly in fear that I may be making the same kind of idiot of myself as the narrator in the story. The story warns not only me but any critic.

Thurber's comedy shows how the meddling, abstract intellect—

of which the critic is a typical embodiment—is comic because it denies the facts of a rich and palpitating life. Thurber's joke about himself, that behind his six-foot figure and his twenty-five books is nothing but a "pussy cat," is a version of this point: the critic will leap to the simple explanation of the pussy cat and thus miss the real complication and the real comedy. He is explaining for us in a comically inappropriate explanation. *Let Your Mind Alone*, a collection of essays on the psychologists' solutions to human problems, hilariously displays the gulf between psychologists who explain and the men and women who live. Our great pleasure in Harold Ross, the *New Yorker* editor, stems from the fact that Ross defies every rational and critical precept about what an editor should be. Margery Albright and Mary Agnes Thurber, the two heroines of *The Thurber Album*, understand life better than doctors, nurses, politicians, and college graduates. The ordinary man, Thurber's comedy says, will understand better than heavy-footed critics with schema and systems.

Despite all the acid comments about critics and criticism, Thurber's comedy shows a strong underlying awareness of the desperate need for felt understanding. It is not that he is opposed to the intellect's search for understanding. The trouble, as he sees it, is that feeling and understanding may get separated. He lowers the large "No Entrance" signs just slightly when he praises intelligence and art as the sole justification of human history. If intellect is dangerous (because it wants to substitute explanations for experience), intelligence, on the other hand, has some value if it is feelingly known. In an essay he wrote for Clifton Fadiman's anthology, *I Believe: The Personal Philosophies of Certain Eminent Men and Women of Our Time* (1939), Thurber affirms that a great deal must be said for intelligence: "It has produced Genius and out of Genius has come art, the one achievement of Man which has made the long trip up from all fours seem well-advised." He consistently praises the same quality of mind—the creative/making power of the imagination—that Wordsworth and Coleridge celebrate in their solemn works.

In the essay for Fadiman's book, Thurber continues,

> Abstract reasoning, itself, has not benefited Man so much as instinct has benefited the lower animals. . . . Instinct has been defined as a "tendency to actions which lead to the attainment of

some goal natural to the species." In giving up instinct and going in for reasoning, Man has aspired higher than the attainment of natural goals; he has developed ideas and notions; he has monkeyed around with concepts. . . . [He] has become the least well-adjusted of all the creatures of the earth, and hence the most bewildered. . . . [Man's] mistaken selection of reason as an instrument of perception has put him in a fine quandary.

Thurber's words in Fadiman's anthology say in dull prose what his sketches show, that the mind is an imperfect tool. The mind makes mistakes or finds explanations that make as much sense as the words "pussy cat." The sketches repeatedly show that the greatest threat to the modern world is the man who uses intellect to control and dominate behavior for his own comfort; thus the comic voice of *Is Sex Necessary?* complains when intellect persuades pretty girls to collect "books on abnormal psychology" but "almost no pretty underwear." The imaginative intelligence — which is to humans what instinct is to animals — will make the necessary connections between brain (psychology) and experience (underwear). To avoid the Thurber lash, we dare not repeat the critical judgments of psychiatrists, Marxists, or anyone else merely embroidering them with the skeins of our own prejudices, as Thurber accuses a character named Charles Endless of doing in a sketch called "*What* Cocktail Party?" (*Thurber Country*). In this sketch, Thurber talks to an endless series of demi-brains all trying to reduce Eliot's play to a cocktail party quip. A tipsy butler ends the sketch by saying, "It is desolater than you think." The "No Entrance" sign may come down just slightly if we avoid approaching Thurber with any conventional cubby-holes or quips. Thurber requires his reader to see him with the same quality of felt understanding that his best sketches dramatize.

If Thurber's own "No Entrance" sign is forbidding enough, our literary climate has a more threatening one. We have no way of saying what is good or bad about comedy. For most of us, a comedy is good if we laugh and not good if we do not laugh. The criterion is not the worst in the world, but the kind of laughter is so varied — from secret twinges to belly laughs — that the criterion is not helpful. Thurber's few critics compare him to Conrad, James, E. B. White, T. S. Eliot and others; these comparisons are useful and I will make some too, but the comparison must illuminate

the comedy and not just *be* for its own sake. Moreover, critics
apologize for comedy. Typically they convert comic writers into
satirists (because they are morally useful), journalists, or something other than a comic artist. When one of Thurber's last stories
was published after his death, I vainly searched the index for it
under the rubrics "Fiction" and "Comedy." It had a category of
its own, "Satire." Malcolm Cowley reviewing a Thurber book in
the 1930's dismissed it because Thurber was not serious about
serious subjects. Both to the ordinary man in the street and to the
critic, comedy is trivial.

Another familiar judgment forbidding criticism of comedy
leaps to every mind thinking about comedy: resist analysis for
fear of losing the heart of the matter. When Wolcott Gibbs reviewed
Max Eastman's *The Enjoyment of Laughter*, he noted that Eastman
told him more about laughter than he wanted to know. It is a good
judgment. By necessity comedy strikes suddenly and swiftly or
it does not strike at all; explain a joke and the joke is gone forever.
If an officious fool tries, stop him. It seems strange, however, that
laughter, a characteristic of our nature that is the same in all lan-
gauges and under all conditions, should be considered beyond
analysis and study. No reviewer of a new astronomical book would
write, "He tells me more about astronomy than I want to know."
Granted, ordinary men may fear that they will lose the beauty of
a night sky if they know the vastness of the universe, but most of
us learn quickly to adjust our knowledge of the universe to our
pleasure in a sky. It may be right to resist an explanation of a
joke, but with the same preparation to accept differences, a good
rule for jokes becomes a bad rule for comedy. Therefore, believing
that comedy of Thurber's kind is almost unstudied, I propose to
look rigorously and fully at his style and grammar. The examination will improve no one's sense of humor, but it may show that
Thurber's comedy casts a wider net and yields greater pleasure
than conventional views suppose.

As usual, Thurber defends himself. In "The Tyranny of Trivia"
(*Lanterns and Lances*), Thurber answers Otto Friedrich's objection
that he indulges in trivia as follows:

> Trivia Mundi has always been as dear and as necessary to me as
> her bigger and more glamorous sister, Gloria. They have both
> long and amicably inhabited a phrase of Coleridge's, "All things

both great and small," and I like to think of them taking turns at
shooting albatrosses and playing the bassoon.

I am grateful that Thurber opts for the bassoon. What I need,
however, is a way of knowing what his choice of the bassoon
means. I need a method which will enable me to see the characteristic design of comedy in his work on the one hand and the
variety and departure from that design on the other hand. For
paradoxically, in the very act of perceiving a design we become
aware of just how much is not encompassed by it. In seeking out
the design of comedy and then seeing how it appears in Thurber's
work we may come to see how witty, how unobtrusive, and how
skillful are the tricks of Thurber's trade.

As a grammar or method for looking at Thurber's comedy,
here are five short statements about what happens in comedy.
They are not original, having been distilled from many comments
on the name and nature of comedy. If they are accurate they will
prove helpful in showing us how the experience of comedy feels.
But it must be said that Thurber's comedy, like any successful
comedy, displays variations on the design — variations that surprise and delight the reader. Surprise and delight are the qualities
that give comedy its life and interest; it is impossible to conceive
of comedy without them. Comic writers create expectations and
then, to our great delight, belie these expectations. In the endings
of his stories, Thurber's characters surprise us by celebrating
tiny, unnoticed private victories instead of the public marriage and
triumphs of older comedy. This variation is significant, for it helps
to distinguish the particular pleasure to be discovered in Thurber.

In addition to the basic element of surprise, comedy does five
other things. (1) Comedy celebrates the victory of witty man over
the obstacles of chance and fortune; it celebrates a vital surge of
felt life. Hence our pleasure in the happy ending. Our word *comedy*
comes from the Greek word *comos*, standing for the marriage
hymn that accompanied the bawdy dance at the end of the Greek
rite of spring. Thurber's handling of this conventional expectation
is not only his most brilliant accomplishment, but also the key to
the changing pattern in his comedy. (2) Comedy deliberately encourages us to think about aspects of life that we try to ignore or
that society wants us to ignore. It loves to puncture sacred cows.

We feel a tension or excitement when a comedian audaciously insults public officials or when he teases us by forays into sex or funerals. If, as Freud suggests, laughter is a release from the tension of society, then the comic writer will deliberately choose subjects to create this tension or excitement. Again Thurber's subjects not only vary from our expectation (in addition to sex, he chooses scientism and efficiency), but also reveal much about his developing power as an artist. (3) Comedy also arises when any law, habit, custom, or quirk is continued beyond what is ordinarily considered as normal or appropriate. We laugh at the repeated "pocketa-pocketa" of Mitty's automobile that is transformed into the "pocketa-pocketa" of an airplane motor because Mitty is stuck in a "humor," rigidly bound to a quirk of his own nature which makes him daydream instead of function according to normal suburban expectations. (4) Comedy occurs when we recognize that an apparent behavior or an apparent truth is not what it seems to be. Disguise is funny the moment we recognize the incongruity between the real man and the appearance of the mask. (5) Comedy praises admirable qualities in society by laughing *with* them and condemns violations of what is socially appropriate by laughing *at* them. Thus our laughter at an actor in a strange costume tells him and us to conform to the notions of appropriate dress. When we laugh at a man speaking a dialect, we force him and other dialect speakers to conform to our notion of appropriate language. By giving its successful characters the dress and language considered admirable, comedy enforces admirable social qualities. Thus comedy shapes and modifies its audience, though to what degree it succeeds is difficult to assess. Comic writers frequently speak of their desire to "correct" man's knowledge or behavior. Thurber, for example, says much about improving taste and intelligence. Finally, since the essence of comedy is unpredictability and surprise, each of these actions of comedy that I list must astound us if it is to be genuinely comic. Comedy must do all of these things and yet not seem to do them; it is a difficult and sophisticated art form.

I illustrate these five statements at a simple and obvious level. Any comic effort, from the music hall joke to the sophisticated comedy of manners to the *Divine Comedy* itself, employs all five. In simple comedy, the action exists merely to provoke laughter;

in more conscious and artistic comedy modes develop and change as a musical line in a symphony develops and changes. Thurber sets an idea completely upside down or plays it straight. In *Is Sex Necessary?* he and White laugh at owlish books of marital advice and the mania to reduce behavior to simplified psychological explanations (she left her husband because she was toilet trained too early). Later he advances from laughter at marriage experts and parlor scientists to attack science (and scientism) itself; he then writes comedy on our method of knowing and understanding our world. From initial laughter at a special absurdity of the 1920's and 1930's, he goes on to laugh at our epistemology, our metaphysics, and even our theology. We can sense the development and complexity of Thurber's comedy with the aid of the norm, the pattern, or expectation which the five statements create. Thurber claimed that he rewrote as many as twenty-five times before he was satisfied; these five statements are a tool to help us understand what comic ideal all those laborious revisions were striving to attain. Therefore, although our general attitude is that comedy cannot be studied and although Thurber himself ridicules criticism, it is possible to speak about comedy without beating the subject to death. What the reader needs to do is to "feel" an understanding.

If Thurber is a writer striving toward the realization of a felt life, then a reader is bound to ask the question, "Who is doing the feeling?" Thurber's objection to criticism is that in its haste to generalize it ignores the special and unique qualities which make genius what it is. In his book on Ross, he says that the only word to communicate the idea of Ross is the word *Ross* itself. The only word to communicate Thurber, then, would be the word *Thurber*. Many of the sketches are spoken by a narrator whom we identify as Thurber himself; he uses his own experience with maids, automobiles, and obtuse women. His best pieces have an autobiographical energy, a desire to probe into his own experience to reshape it and to discover in it the springs of action. The two books I praise most, *The Thurber Album* and *The Years with Ross* are as autobiographical as James Joyce's *A Portrait of the Artist as a Young Man* or Wordsworth's *Prelude*. Even named characters in his fiction are, often, writers like him who live in suburban Connecticut and have many of his traits (except for his blindness, a matter discussed only in the openly biographical pieces). For anyone who thinks that the proper study of Thurber is Thurber himself, he has written sufficient rebuttal in pieces called "Memoirs of a Drudge," "The Notebooks of James Thurber," and many others. The key to understanding a writer is not in the minutiae remaining after a life is over.

Certain known facts, however, ought to be presented even if they supply no magic key, no Figure in the Carpet. He was born and grew up in Columbus, Ohio, in what might seem, on the surface, an ordinary middle-class family of father, mother, and three sons. The one outwardly remarkable event of his childhood (he writes of astonishing inward events) was the injury of one eye during a childhood game. Because of his bad eyesight, he was not drafted during the First World War but stayed at The Ohio State University until 1918 when he left, without taking his degree, to go to Paris as a code clerk for the State Department. Like many other men of his generation, he mulled over the experience in Paris and the time of the war; one event during that time is told in three different versions and one of his last stories narrates a return to Paris and a remembrance of things that had happened in 1918.

After leaving government service, he returned to Columbus where he wrote for the *Dispatch*, the major newspaper in the city. He married in 1922 and three years later went to France to write a novel. In contrast to the years in Paris, he rarely speaks of these years in Columbus when he was not only a working journalist but the author of annual revues performed by the students at the University. He left the provincial newspaper and the college theater to try writing a novel, but because he failed (he later said) to get beyond five thousand words, he reported for the *Chicago Tribune*. Returning to New York, he worked for the New York *Evening Post* and wrote a 25,000 word parody "Why We Behave Like Microbe Hunters," which was rejected by publishers and evidently has not survived in manuscript. He also began to get his first acceptances by the *New Yorker*. In 1927 he joined the staff of that magazine. After a short tenure as managing editor, he joined E. B. White and Wolcott Gibbs in writing the "Talk of the Town" section. Thurber writes about his experiences in the 1920's reluctantly and only in fragments. One imagines him as a bright young newspaperman, possibly writing with just a little more brio than his fellows but still a man who has not quite caught a way of speaking. He tells of long labor that was unsuccessful and of how the first story that he sold to the *New Yorker* was actually dashed off in less than an hour. He apprenticed himself to the newspapers, the college theater, and finally to E. B. White; it is a period of withdrawal, but it must have been absolutely essential to his growth as a writer.

If the 1920's were his period of trial, in the 1930's he began to succeed. He published a book every two years, and the *New Yorker* is full of the work from which he culls the pieces to be put into the books. His only child, a daughter, was born in 1931, but his first marriage ended in 1935 and he then married Helen Wismer. After 1935, he could afford to free-lance, but the *New Yorker*, having first refusal, published most of his material. His eyesight, never strong, was complicated by cataract operations beginning in 1940 which, however, failed to halt the progressive loss of sight. Thurber commented to an interviewer that the imagination does not go blind, and indeed he begins his most creative period when the problem of his eyes is most aggravated. He lived in Connecticut, far enough away to avoid city distractions but close enough to enjoy metropolitan attractions. In the 1920's and the 1930's he was both close to and yet distant from events and people. He was in Paris immediately after the war, but he was a civilian. He returned in 1925 at the very height of the American invasion of Paris, and yet he seems not to have participated in that invasion in the way that Hemingway, Fitzgerald and other Americans did. He lived in New York during the depression, but earned a comfortable living. He rarely speaks of political, cultural, or social events in the passionate and committed style of Dos Passos or Steinbeck or Clifford Odets. He knew Humphrey Bogart, Franchot Tone, Hemingway, Dorothy Parker, and John McNulty; his book *The Years with Ross* is filled with letters from and conversations with men as varying as Edmund Wilson and Ogden Nash. He was the first American since Mark Twain to be invited to the editorial table of *Punch*. Unlike others of his generation, Thurber recollects this material in tranquility. He makes neither naked nor frontal assaults to report life in newspaper rooms or in bohemian garrets. He is more apt to describe raising a dog in the city. In the Preface to *My Life and Hard Times* he says that he writes neither about Walter Lippmann's time nor Professor Einstein's time, but

> his own personal time, circumscribed by the short boundaries of his pain and his embarrassment, in which what happens to his digestion, the rear axle of his car, and the confused flow of his relationships with six or eight persons and two or three buildings is of greater importance than what goes on in the nation or in the universe. He knows vaguely that the nation is not much good any more; he has read that the crust of the earth is shrinking alarmingly and that the universe is growing steadily colder, but he does not believe that any of the three is in half as bad shape as he is.

But if it is his own personal time, it is more remarkably like the time of other men, observing and afraid, than it is a time unique in social or political happening.

His experience is transmuted into his books where it can be shaped and formed by the detached but observing comic artist. Comedy, we say, requires distance from its subjects; it is easy to laugh about things when we are not involved. ". . . [the] confusions and the panics of last year and the year before," he writes in the same Preface to *My Life and Hard Times*, "are too close for contentment." The panics of last year are too close for comedy and he seldom writes about last year. In Thurber, distance permits a faint tinge of rose around the events of his melancholy time and thus, marvelously, makes comedy out of what had been too deeply felt for tears. His life does offer certain clues: his experience as a reporter must have taught him a little about the English sentence and he says that White taught him more; the *New Yorker* developed its style at the same time that Thurber did his and it is hard to know which influenced which more; the Thurber woman changed slightly, but clearly, and his own marriage changed slightly but clearly. Nevertheless, it is not in the confusions and panics of his life, but in his books that we find the fascinating version of that life.

He transmuted the facts of his life into his art, and his art is the major consideration. He created a character named Thurber in his sketches. Interviewers always reported that the man they met surprised them, for each interviewer had expected the man who exists in the fiction. To understand and enjoy Thurber, we do not need to know the real man but we need to know the man who appears in his work. The materials for the life are not available to readers now, but what is available are twenty-five books, one play, three collections of drawings, and the revue.

I have two convictions about James Thurber. The first is that his comic form provides him with a perspective to view the confusion of the twentieth century and make it meaningful. The second follows directly: that therefore his form needs serious study. The first conviction, that his comic form is peculiarly necessary, is evident the minute one compares Thurber's career with that of nearly any other American writer in the twentieth century. In "The Waters of the Moon" (*The Beast in Me*) Thurber makes comedy out of the fact that American writers "have the occupational span of a hockey player," they go stale or peter out when they turn fifty. One explanation is that the American writer, to whom experience is frequently preliminary to his form, ceases to write when his body can no longer participate. If the American writer has a typical limitation, it is that he often fails to encompass his material in significant form. When he can no longer experience, and since he has a tenuous concept of form, he can no longer write. Thurber has the comic form to sustain him and he continues to write very well into his sixties. He sometimes falters, but then all men falter and at all times in their lives. Early in his career Thurber found out how to use the form of comedy and how to develop it as a better and better instrument. He was fifty-six when he wrote "The Waters of the Moon" and it is a joy. Thurber, unlike so many others, does not burn out. In his last decade, he frequently writes better than he ever wrote, and his improvement is especially clear when the criterion for judgment derives from a study of his whole work. The second conviction follows as the night the day: we must understand his sketches, stories, and essays against the comic tradition. Putting him into that tradition is not simple and requires a new language to name unnamed features of that tradition. Learning a new language is hard, but the result is the discovery of a new world. To learn the language of Thurber's comedy is to discover how much he accomplished and how much he developed what he received. If the reader can observe Thurber's variations of the comic ending, the tension of his comic attack, the method of repeating a habit or custom for comic statement, the incongruity between appearance and reality, and the comic distance that enables us to laugh at social vanities, then he is ready to see that Thurber indeed created a pleasure dome of the American imagination. The view from his dome changes the life of our ordinary experience below. He gives us clarity in his vision and thoroughness. He presents a challenge which I do not choose to ignore.

II

❊

The Subjects of Comedy

There is a long tradition that tells us to denigrate comedy. Aristotle, trying to piece together his response to the Greek theater, observed "there are no early records of comedy, because it was not highly valued." Indeed, Aristotle's own examination of comedy disappeared into the mists of time, surviving only in an Arabic summary that does not tell much about comedy or what Aristotle really thought. E. B. White repeats the Greek philosopher and finds too that the world undervalues the comic vision:

> The world likes humor, but it treats it patronizingly. It decorates its serious artists with laurel, and its wags with Brussels sprouts. It feels that if a thing is funny it can be presumed to be something less than great, because if it were truly great it would be wholly serious. Writers know this, and those who take their literary selves with great seriousness are at considerable pains never to associate their name with anything funny or flippant or nonsensical or "light." They suspect it would hurt their reputation, and they are right. Many a poet writing today signs his real name to his serious verse and a pseudonym to his comical verse, being unwilling to have the public discover him in any way but a pensive and heavy moment. It is a wise precaution. (It is often a bad poet, too.)

Post-Puritan America, I suspect, takes White at face value. Thurber himself argues that "The modern morbid playwrights seem to have fallen for the fake argument that only tragedy is serious and has importance, whereas the truth is that comedy is just as important, and often more serious in its approach to truth, and, what few writers seem to realize or admit, usually more difficult to write." Both Thurber and White protest too much. We are all familiar with the comic actor who insists that he wants to play *Hamlet*—and who gets a laugh at the suggestion. The fact remains, however, that Thurber's first two books, *Is Sex Necessary?* (1929) and *The Owl in the Attic* (1931) are excellent examples of how the comic writer uses what might be called serious and important subjects for his own comic ends. Part of the great delight in these books is our instinctive recognition that the lugubrious topics and even situations are transmogrified (to use a comic word) into subjects fit and proper for laughter. In these two books Thurber finds his subject—the human feeling for life, the evil of machines, the quest for meaning, and the strong vitality of the female—and puts the subjects into the distant world of comedy where we can celebrate their seriousness by laughing at them. There is no contradiction.

The first book, *Is Sex Necessary? Or Why You Feel The Way You Do*, has a perfectly serious subject which is, therefore, a fit subject for laughter.* We cannot laugh at things we do not care about and clearly we must care about this subject. His second book, *The Owl in the Attic*, begins with eight sketches about Mr. and Mrs. Monroe. The hero of these pieces finds himself in such pitiable situations that the reader tempers his laughter by the "shock of recognition," for there he stands and, if it were not for the comic tone, he would not laugh at all. The other two sections of *The Owl in the Attic*, "Pet Department" and "Ladies' and Gentlemen's Guide to Modern English Usage," take a healthy grip on patent idiocies about meaning and grammar to make them subjects for the comic.

*Although the book is a collaboration with E. B. White, it is not difficult to determine which part of it is Thurber's. White says, in an introduction to a paperback reprint, that the first chapter, "The Nature of the American Male: A Study of Pedestalism," is Thurber's. Robert M. Coates, a close friend of both men (Thurber dedicated his third book to him), says that Thurber wrote alternate chapters. I conclude that the Preface (White wrote the Foreword) and the first, third, fifth, and seventh chapters belong to Thurber. In this chapter I discuss only these portions of the book.

The Comedy of the Human Condition

Is Sex Necessary? purports to be a heavy and painstaking analysis of sex. According to Robert Coates, the book sold 40,000 copies in 1929; I suspect the motives of half the people who bought it. White says, in his "Introduction" to a recent paperback edition, that during the war, when the book appeared in an Armed Forces edition, soldiers wrote from overseas to ask, "What's all this—we don't get it." The only reply is the punch line of the Jewish comedian, "You expected something else, maybe?" The subject is interesting, and to judge by the plethora of marriage manuals, magazine articles, and just plain talk, it is relevant. Since the conventional prescriptions for behavior are gone, man cannot turn with certainty to the inherited truths and habits. He turns to pedantic and abstruse analyses by "sociologists, analysts, gynecologists, psychologists, and authors." Sex, Thurber writes, was biology to the Chinese and economics on the American frontier, but now it has become a matter of the *psyche*, whatever that is. Precisely in the collision between the old Puritan ethic, with its denial of pleasure and stern injunctions about behavior, and the new Freudian insight, with its approval of pleasure and its dispensation to enjoy, lies a rich area for comedy. Thurber writes,

> At the turn of the century, the nation was on a sound economic basis and men had the opportunity to direct their attention away from the mechanics of life to the pleasures of living. No race can leap lightly, however, from an economic value to an emotional value.

This statement, with its conjunction of economics and emotions, is both funny and true; the combination is a powerful incentive to keep reading to see how sex looks when it is connected to economics.

Thurber's contributions offer another incentive. More than White in his chapters, Thurber indulges his strong inclination to write vignettes. He dramatizes his little painful situations and shows us men running wildly amuck trying to put the psychologists' lessons into some kind of meaningful practice. White, more the essayist, keeps his illustrations within his essay idea, but Thurber digresses into strange and divergent byways before he brings the reader back to his starting point. Some of the vignettes could be pulled out of their context (I would not recommend it) and published as short stories. In these little subsidiary dramas, Thurber shows us the alienated modern man, the stumbling rationalistic mind, and the futile quest for meaning. He demonstrates also his conviction of the superior vitality of women; his female characters all have perfect control of their destinies, but his men come to utter confusion and impotence. Thurber's men, to use the words of another poet, end not with a bang but with a whimper.

These endings — with all the paraphernalia of confusion and impotence — surprise us. We expect comic heroes to discover order and meaning. The Greek comedies end in marriages, but Thurber's men rarely get to the marriage bed, and when they do, the results are hardly worth celebrating. Consider the sad but funny story of George Smith, used to illustrate a point in the chapter entitled "The Nature of the American Male." George Smith is the first of Thurber's Prufrock characters; he is a paradigm of modern man alienated from his society, isolated from his fellow man, and scared. Having attained the age of thirty-two, George Smith, real estate operator, has "freed his libido without difficulty from familiar objects, and [is] eager to marry." In a world that allows him time to think about sex as sex (and not as biological or economic fact), poor George is frustrated by the Delay Mechanism that modern woman has at her fingertips. She makes fudge; she plays cards; she plays kissing games. Thus frustrated, most American men retreat to their den and to hobbies as harmless sex substitutes. George, however, becomes incredibly involved in a sex substitute, a game of pigs-in-clover which he cannot solve. As one of the psychologists Thurber burlesques would say, he loses his function as a human being. Worse, his game proves as unsuccessful as his pursuit of the young lady; he cannot get the three little balls into their proper holes. George is thoroughly displaced. Because he cannot marry, he is isolated from his society. He is the man who represents, in Matthew Arnold's description of the type, "the utmost calamity, . . .the liveliest anguish, a suffering [which] finds no vent in action; in which a continuous state of mental distress is prolonged, unrelieved by incident, hope, or resistance; in which there is everything to be endured, nothing to be done." [Matthew Arnold, "Preface" to *Poems* (1853) in *The Complete Prose Works of Matthew Arnold*, ed. R. H. Super, Vol. I (Ann

Arbor, 1960), 2-3.] Arnold was being highly serious in his description of an alienated modern man, but Thurber makes his man funny because George Smith's continuous state of mental distress is not a question of the Trinity but a pigs-in-clover puzzle and a woman who makes fudge!

George Smith's three attempted solutions to his dilemma become increasingly comic as the essay progresses: (1) he tries games as a substitute for sex, (2) he tries scientific experiments, and (3) he finds himself in the hands of an extremely obtuse analyst. For his first solution, Smith withdraws to his den to solve the pigs-in-clover puzzle. Thurber has previously explained that games in dens are retreats from sexual frustrations. The den he describes is, in small, an example of God's own junkyard, or, to be more grand, the modern wasteland. It contains, in part,

> a paper-weight from Lookout Mountain, a jagged shell from Chickamaugua, a piece of wood from the *Maine*, . . .a letter-opener from Niagara Falls, . . .a musket-badge from the G. A. R. parade, a red tumbler from the state fair, a photograph of Julia Marlowe, a monk's head match-holder, a Malay kriss, five pipe racks, a shark's tooth, a starfish, a snapshot of the owner's father's bowling team, colored pictures of Natural Bridge and Balanced Rock, a leather table runner with an Indian chief on it, and the spangled jacket of a masquerade costume, softly shedding its sequins.

George Smith's withdrawal to his den to ponder and fiddle and make Unconscious Drawings is a comic example of the vacuum that is modern life. Almost prophetically Thurber employs a symbol that soon afterwards acquired an unexpected power. Thurber says that in the den, Smith "thought up childish diversions. . .and to justify his absorption in these futile pastimes he exaggerated their importance." He continues by noting that in his junkyard, in the landscape of the modern world, nothing happens in "art, science, or engineering."

> Art, indeed, consisted chiefly of putting strange devices on boxes with the aid of a wood-burning set. The commonest device was the swastika, whose curiously distorted conformation bears no discernible relationship to any known phallic symbolism. Those years were blank, idle, lost years.

One's breath is taken away.

It does not help Thurber's comedy, however, that within four years the Nazis had seized power in Germany and made his joke painful. Thurber could well have constructed a more plangent and even pertinent joke by having George draw the burning crosses and hooded figures of the Ku Klux Klan. Or he could have used the symbols of any other group that derives its power by exploiting the fears of frustrated, alienated George Smiths. To use a familiar symbol would be disastrous to comedy. He chose the symbol of what in 1929 was still a little-known splinter group in Germany. The swastika is an ancient symbol used widely in Europe and among American Indians. It was known, yet foreign enough not to engage particular emotions. By an accident of history, Thurber's joke was destroyed. One's breath is taken away; one does not laugh.

George's second response is equally breath-taking, and again it is so breath-taking that the comedy may utterly disappear except in wry, familiar recognition of our pain. He rounds up eighty-five per cent of the dogs in Indianapolis on the theory that one of the dogs ought to be sagacious enough to grasp the idea of the pigs-in-clover puzzle. He makes a speech to them; "Fifty or more St. Bernards and a few dozen Chesapeake spaniels listened, half-heartedly, but the others made holiday." George has a job to do and he is determined. His "Justification of Occupation. . .took the form of exaggerating the importance of finding out whether the puzzle could possibly be solved, and of working out a methodology of solving it more readily." The important word is *methodology*. He has learned a great deal from his society. George is locked in a pointless and futile activity. His mother goes to French Lick in a run-down condition; he pays no attention to his job. Our laughter at George Smith is tempered by the sudden, chilling awareness that his behavior has some of the overtones of what we have seen on assembly lines or in newsreels of masses of stern and determined soldiers. But unlike Thurber's use of the swastika, his mad story about the dogs is still in the cuckoo-land of comedy rather than in the painful world of experience. Because George's compulsive, unthinking action has only the overtones but not the actual form of the assembly line, his comedy can sustain itself. For my taste it is superior to Chaplin's exploitation of a similar theme in the assembly line scene from *Modern Times*, because Chaplin comes close to producing the same effect as Thurber did by using the swastika.

Third, George receives help from a psychologist. Or rather, a psychologist uses his blundering techniques to divert George's "Magnification of Objective, first by Analytic Reasoning, and then by cold application." In short, Smith is to take a cold shower, that famous middle-western solution to "pother" (a word defined in the glossary as "Uncalled-for interest in something—almost always sex"). George, however, has no time for cold applications or Analytic Reasoning; half the dogs, remember, are still making a holiday. Accidentally he drops one of the puzzles:

> He then found that he did not have to roll the balls into the opening, *but could push them with his finger.* He got a hammer and broke the glass in all the thousands of puzzles he had brought to his home for the dogs, and solved every one of the puzzles by pushing, not rolling. This instantly released him from his complex by the Gordian Knot principle of complex release. He thus gained the necessary confidence and sense of power to feel worthy of the woman with whom he was in love, and he finally married her. The marriage was of average success.

And thus he escapes from his anguish and suffering, but he does not escape with the resounding joy and celebration of older comedy. He squeaks out, accidentally, and the marriage, the expected mark of his triumph, is just one of average success. The story might be called "The Lovesong of J. Alfred Smith of Indianapolis."

I give the story of George Smith so fully because he is the first example of the feeling understanding, a subject that occupies Thurber throughout his comedy. Repeatedly modern man gets himself trapped in such self-created dilemmas as George Smith's puzzle problem. Man is always monkeying around with concepts and has thus become the least well-adjusted and most bewildered of creatures with eighty-five per cent of the dogs and two psychologists unable to help. Finally it is feeling, enlightened understanding, George Smith's own human nature that discover the solution. Neither games, technology (his experiment with the dogs), nor science could help, but his own nature accidentally leads him to rediscover his function as a human being. In Thur-

ber's prose, the individual is best off when he is freed of all the
paraphernalia of systems, whether mechanical, social, literary or
just plain transcendental.

In addition to this specific ridicule of systems in the story of
George Smith, the whole book ridicules the notion of viewing
human experience from the stance of dull, obtuse, stupid scientism. *Is Sex Necessary?* is spoken by a *persona*, an assumed personality supposedly representing two scientific students of sex
who are reporting their findings, (at one point Thurber refers to
his colleague Dr. White). Part of the joke is that the scientific mind
is so colorless that both men write the same stultifying objective
jargon. The speaker, representative of his type, is obtuse: he almost completely lacks common sense, and is totally unsuccessful
in his efforts to reduce human experience to abstract and absolute
law. In his "Discussion of Feminine Types" he is ridiculously
unable to interpret the commonest social relationship. He betrays
his lack of common sense and humanity when, on a Fifth Avenue
bus, he approaches a woman whom he has followed and observed
for several weeks. He says, "Madam. . .I would greatly appreciate
making a leisurely examination of you, at your convenience." The
woman struck him "and descended at the next even-numbered
street — Thirty-sixth, I believe it was." If George Smith is the primitive model of the Thurber man who will achieve full expression
in Walter Mitty and the heroes of the fairy tales, the *persona* of
Is Sex Necessary? is a model of the thick-headed, chill and un-
imaginative man who dominates some of the stories he wrote at
the end of his career. The threat of the *persona* is the threat of
mindless application of abstract clichés. His subject is both necessary and comic.

Is Sex Necessary? also includes Thurber's initial foray into
the question of meaning in language, a question fit for comedy,
tragedy, and philosophy. In a world cut off from experience by
jargon and stereotyped pap, the sense behind words is sometimes
all but unattainable. In this first book Thurber dramatizes the
difficulties compounded on a marriage night by

> A young lady whose silly mother had taught her to believe that
> she would have a little son, three years old, named Ronald, as
> soon as her husband brought a pair of bluebirds into a room
> filled with lilies-of-the-valley.

The *persona* reduces the situation to a "case" of "Birds and Flowers Fixation." The young man and woman unsuccessfully try to communicate. He tries to explain in French, but becomes hopelessly tangled in personal and impersonal pronouns. They switch to archaic English, but even then the pronouns are too complex. Again games and science offer pointless outlet to the functionless man. If the difficulty of language is not overcome, then

> The home becomes a curious sort of hybrid, with overtones of the botanical garden and the aviary. The husband grows morose and snappish, the wife cross and pettish. Very often she takes up lacrosse and he goes in for raising rabbits. If allowed to go on, the situation can become so involved and intricate that not all the analysts from the time of Joan of Arc down could unravel it.

From the comic exploitation of non-meaning, Thurber is only a slight step away from the outrageous word games in some of his later pieces. Always at our back we hear the philosophers in their great debates on the meaning of meaning and the critics worrying over the many types of ambiguity.

Another subject which the book examines is the superior vitality of the female. The vitality springs from woman's greater intuition, and her greater sense of fact. She is not usually as deluded as the young woman with the Birds and Flowers Fixation. The point is acted out in "Claustrophobia, or What Every Young Wife Should Know." After a horrifying example of a husband being "boxed in" by his wife's interest in the objects of her home, the psychologist-*persona* gives wives instruction on how to lead a husband to the essential facts of life: how to tell him about guest towels, how to teach him to unpack, and how to give him a sense of freedom while taking freedom away. Only men suffer in Thurber's world; women, because of their greater contact with experience, because of their intuition, serenely ride the crest of life. Men require conventions, abstractions, concepts which stand between them and experience, but his women need no filter or screen. Thurber women do not take showers to escape from compulsions and fixations. Late in his career, Thurber praises his mother's ability to create chaos and confusion because she is more concerned for the felt quality of life than any "boxing in" that men require.

Because he chooses subjects that even the most dull and un-imaginative reader would find interesting, Thurber's comedy is worthy of attention. He puts into his comic vision the revolution in science and technology and the man who seems to have lost his human function as a result of these. At the same time that he is comic, he is serious in his approach to truth, for he sees that technology, science, and great proliferation of wealth are useless until the George Smiths of the world break the glass and push the little balls with their fingers, until ladies with Birds and Flower Fixations manage to see the facts of life.

The Thin Line between Comedy and Pathos

The modes of comedy and tragedy interplay in the "Mr. and Mrs. Monroe" sketches which open Thurber's second book, *The Owl in the Attic* (1931). In the figure of Mr. Monroe the comedy comes tantalizingly close to the tragic vision since he experiences both despair and catastrophe. The sketches have no continued plot in the sense that the hero faces a focused opposition over which he eventually triumphs. He faces, rather, seemingly unrelated predicaments. The sketches seem to have a time movement so that we sense Mr. Monroe's increasing age. We see Mr. Monroe first as a young man at a party and last as a middle-aged man deciding to go back to sleep instead of venturing forth to attempt a clandestine seduction. The sketches have a further movement in that the husband becomes increasingly unable to cope with his predicaments. If comedy is ordinarily a work in which young men triumph (the resurrected hero in Greek comedy actually is a young man who begins as an old man as the comedy opens) and if it is a movement toward reuniting a hero with his society, then Mr. Monroe is hardly a fit comic hero. A man too sleepy to go awooing reverses the comic hero's usual role. Not only is he in despair, but he constantly suffers catastrophes. He is socially embarrassed by his wife's slightly drunken behavior at a sedate tea party. Pursued by shouts he runs from a pier carrying three bottles of smuggled Benedictine in a hat box (though the shouts of his pursuers are only a man calling a taxi). He spends a night on a cold hallway couch, and he misses his rendezvous with a complaisant lady.

The poor fool has more potential for pathos than comedy, but his frightening and agonizing situations are more extreme than that and thus comic. Further, the situations also suggest that behind the comic mask is a raw human experience which the writer, by his craft, has subdued for our pleasure. What is painful in life is transformed into a finer tone by the comic vision.

That same comic vision, however, occasionally dissatisfies because the denouement of comedy is necessarily fixed. A lesser comic writer would allow Mr. Monroe to find some saving loophole to keep his delusions intact. The fact that he never escapes from his predicaments, paradoxically, makes him funny. We have an additional unexpected complication that we had not expected.

Another unexpected complication is the behavior of little Mrs. Monroe. She is always called "little" in the sketches, yet she always triumphs. Typically in comedy a male defeats an enemy and then wins the female as his prize. In Thurber's story, the female defeats the enemy and the male has his prize by default. Even her husband's domesticity—he goes to sleep, significantly, over James's *The Golden Bowl*—reflects her power to outwit opposing forces. Mrs. Monroe has tamed her husband; she has followed the advice of the mock psychologist in *Is Sex Necessary?* and given him only enough freedom to think that he has some. In "The 'Wooing' of Mr. Monroe," his wife destroys the threat to her marriage by paying a social call on her rival and recounting a ludicrous story about her husband's losing battle with a shower faucet. Although he is victimized by moving men, noises that go bump in the night, and the intricacies of railroad terminals, little Mrs. Monroe remains undaunted by terrors. If the extremity of Mr. Monroe's pain suggests comedy, the energy of his wife moves us across the thin line from actual pain into the pleasure of comic complications.

Still Mr. Monroe is a comic hero. Our attention goes to him and we feel a kind of resurrection and triumph as he lies in bed and goes to sleep with his illusion still intact. He is a modern Quixote. He reads books and seriously considers "God, ethics, morals, humanism, and so on." Like the original Quixote he cannot meaningfully relate his imperturbable books on higher issues to the chaos of his perplexity. Mrs. Monroe is his Sancho Panza; her vision is obscured neither by the mist of abstract intellect, nor by the fog of Henry James. She instinctively knows what goes

to storage and what should be moved to the country house. She
can get them out of a sedate but boring tea party. But before she
rescues her husband we are aware of his inward sickness, the
countless thwartings of his will. Man laughs, Wylie Sypher says,
(see *Works Consulted*) "only because he can suffer excruciatingly,"
and we laugh at Mr. Monroe because he suffers humiliation, disappointment and chagrin (rather than death) until Mrs. Monroe's
hard sense of fact comes through to provide his moment of resurrection or triumph. Comedy is, Professor L. C. Knights observes,
essentially a serious activity. Because the "Mr. and Mrs. Monroe"
sketches make us so acutely aware of the perplexities, the thwartings of human experience, they please the reader. As in all of Thurber's best sketches, the hint of disaster serves as a foil to the comedy.

Comedy as Criticism

T. S. Eliot's comment on Thurber (as stated in *Time* 58 (9 July,
1951), 88-90) points to another quality of Thurber's comedy which
justifies our attention.

> It is a form of humor which is also a way of saying something
> serious. There is a criticism of life at the bottom of it. It is serious
> and even somber. Unlike so much humor, it is not merely a criti-
> cism of manners—that is, of the superficial aspects of society
> at a given moment—but something more profound.

Comedy is a form of criticism, or evaluation, of the human condition. In fact, at its best, comedy may provide a more thorough
criticism because it is complex and ambiguous. The second and
third sections of *The Owl in the Attic*, "Pet Department" and
"Ladies' and Gentlemen's Guide to Modern English Usage," not
only examine life but also evaluate or criticize it. Not only do these
sections look, but they also judge by giving a clearer sense of the
issue.

The headnote for "Pet Department" says that "The idea for
the department was suggested by the daily pet column in the *New
York Evening Post*, and by several others." Each item prints a
vacuous question from a newspaper reader and an equally vacuous

answer from the reporter. Each correspondent sends a picture of his pet to make the problem more vivid. The questions are stupid questions that could be answered with a modicum of observation, and all the advice is (1) ludicrously inadequate to the situation, even in the abbreviated form given, and (2) pretentiously more than adequate. The editor of the Pet Department knows all of the answers and yet the very fact that he knows all is complete evidence that he knows nothing. Thus Thurber, the critic, challenges formulae that pretentiously fail to account for human or animal peculiarities. He has already challenged the formulae of the analysts who failed to help George Smith, but the challenge in "Pet Department" has the advantage of being placed further from the reader. The discussion of animals has the quality of a disinterested scientific experiment. We consider Thurber's letter-writers and their foolish questions with the detachment of a biologist studying amoebae. One questioner writes about a "gull that cannot get his head down. . .and bumps into things"; the newspaper respondent replies that the owner doesn't have a gull at all but "a rabbit backing up." We are reminded of the oracular advice of the lovelorn columns but also of the busy tendency of our civilization to proliferate specialists who take the task of living away from those who consult them. Not only does the specialist tell his client that he has a rabbit, but he officiously corrects grammar and meddles with the question in an extremely high-handed fashion. Thus we see ourselves oppressed by knowing pedagogues, traffic experts, efficiency experts, and who knows what all. The comic vision permits a displaced examination of the subject; comedy has a more disinterested criticism to make.

Much of the comedy and criticism of "Pet Department" depends upon the observation that animals, who react according to their nature and thus succeed (whereas men act according to abstractions and thus fail), need advice because of human stupidity. Thus, to the question about a dog who appears to be thinking, the supposed newspaper columnist replies:

> Owing to the artificially complex life led by city dogs of the present day, they tend to lose the simpler systems of intuition which once guided all breeds, and frequently lapse into what comes very close to mental perplexity. . . . I would judge that your dog has merely mislaid something and wonders where he put it.

The confusion between the human and animal world illustrates not only the failure of formulae but also the failure of human experience itself to give significant meaning. If experience makes dogs go dotty, what then can it do to humans?

The wit in the "Pet Department" is delightful but no one needs to pay attention; the game of comedy is played because it is an obvious game and we can enjoy it. We must pay attention to his subject in the Mr. and Mrs. Monroe sketches and in "Ladies' and Gentlemen's Guide to Modern English Usage" because Thurber's comedy questions our basic assumptions about life. I can exist without advice on animal behavior, but I cannot exist without language. Like the Monroe sketches, the "Guide" has behind it the pressure of insistent questions. Thurber selects a dangerous topic again; it is risky business to try to outdo a witty man. H. W. Fowler's excellent *A Dictionary of Modern English Usage* has wit and charm of its own. Editors and writers keep copies for the wit even though Fowler's 1926 advice is now somewhat old-fashioned; the book has been twice revised since the original publication that Thurber parodies. Fowler has been revised, but Thurber's comedy never needs revision. His parody does not ridicule (parody is usually a great compliment), but Thurber rather seizes on the comic elements of language usage. As Fowler is a criticism of life (an assumption not denied), so is Thurber. But Fowler is tied down to the language practices of his class and his nation; Thurber is released by his comedy so that his observations have a permanence and relevance not to be found in the original.

The "Guide" parodies Fowler but it uses the grammarian's method to comment on man and social conventions. Though at first blush it may seem extravagant to claim that Thurber is more philosophical than Fowler, he has in fact caught a rhythm that is more universal and consistent. Thurber's article on split infinitives begins by pointing out that hard and fast rules about splitting infinitives are as hard to know as hard and fast rules about striking a lady. Generally one does not strike a lady, but Thurber's narrator immediately recalls the case of a woman who needs to be struck when she has had too much red and white wine at a dinner party. The man who follows the letter of the law and does not strike the lady (or does not split the infinitive) invites a dinner party brawl (or linguistic confusion) when the slightly drunken lady climbs on the table and begins to sing. "There is nothing more deplorable," Thurber writes in the even, reasonable tone of a disinterested student,

> than the spectacle of a formal dinner party ending in a brawl. And yet it is surprising how even the most cultured and charming people can go utterly to pieces when something is unexpectedly thrown at table. . . . Usually this tendency passes as quickly as it comes, but it is astounding how rapidly it can be converted into action once the spell of dignity and well-bred reserve is broken by the sight of, say, a green-glass salad plate flying through the air.

The same chaos may result from over-punctilious care about grammar. Thurber's pieces say that grammar is more complex, funny, and serious than we had suspected.

The evaluation or criticism of the "Guide" parallels the limited criticism of *Is Sex Necessary?* since both works assert that abstract law cannot incorporate human experience. The parody, however, goes even further, noting that abstract law gets fixed in human habit and acquires a caveat all out of proportion to actual conditions. Fowler says the same. Grammar becomes hopelessly involved in medieval speculation somewhere between high school Latin and human experience. The first discussion in the "Guide," on the pitfalls of "Who and Whom," ends:

> Only this, that it is better to use 'whom' when in doubt, and even better to re-word the statement, and leave out all the relative pronouns, except ad, ante, con, in, inter, ob, post, prae, pro, sub, and super.

At this point the New Linguists, scholars seeking to derive a terminology and method for language from spoken practice, enter to correct the error which comedy exploits. The error of describing English as if it were Latin has been long known, but the comic writer uses the error and makes it vivid. Thurber is not, of course, responsible for rewriting English grammar, but he makes a criticism of grammar that is supported in serious and scholarly activity. He does more than use the manners of grammar for comedy; he evaluates the problem of language.

The parodies of Fowler (there are nine) not only communicate the terror of trying to make meaning with language but also the delight in succeeding. To the uncritical, meaning is merely a matter of saying. Meaning, Thurber suggests, is more likely a matter of screaming. "Adverbial Advice" is wrong in its advice, but the article succeeds in making the linguistic point that communication is prior to all forms or rules.

> . . .the sufferer should say, 'I look well, but I don't feel well.' While this usage has the merit of avoiding the troublesome words 'bad' and 'badly,' it also has the disadvantage of being a negative statement. If a person is actually ill, the important thing is to find out not how he doesn't feel, but how he does feel. He should state his symptoms more specifically—'I have a gnawing pain here, that comes and goes,' or something of the sort. There is always the danger, of course, that one's listeners will cut in with a long description of how they feel; this can usually be avoided by screaming.

The instruction—to be specific in positive statements—is eminently sound. It is, as I said, philosophical comedy, and it communicates to any citizen who may think, complacently, that he understands the grammar rag. Thurber opens the eye of understanding, even on the subject of grammar.

Thurber's first two books (or his first book and a half, when we count White as coauthor of the first) humorously examine experience for the sake of laughter, but they go beyond laughter and make us know, in our laughter, the pressure of pain and uncertainty. If comedy is to be genuinely successful, it will use exactly the same material as any other literary form. The stories of George Smith, Mr. Monroe, or the lady who throws plates when she has had too much red and white wine are potentially fit for tragedy, satire, or romance as well as comedy. The sketches in "Pet Department," however, can hardly be conceived as anything but comic sketches; they quite easily became sketches ridiculing television in the Broadway revue, *A Thurber Carnival*. Thurber's work, when he is at his best, illustrates what Wylie Sypher calls "Perhaps the most important discovery in modern criticism, . . .the perception that comedy and tragedy are somehow akin, . . .that comedy can tell us many things about our situation even tragedy cannot." (see *Works Consulted*) Sypher is addressing a general audience that believes tragedy is superior, but I still complain that his emphasis on tragedy is unnecessary. The tragic man is caught in his system; the comic man escapes from his system. *Is Sex Necessary?* has alienated, frustrated George Smith and a husband with a silly wife, but in both cases life asserts itself against the psychologist's abstract systems. Both men escape from their tragic box (not very heroically, it is true, but they get out). Despite all the odds Mr. Monroe avoids the incursions of a menacing and complicated civilization that sometimes treats him better than he expected. Even the system of grammar is a fit subject. Thurber tells us about our situation as fully and seriously as any other writer using any other form. Therefore, "Mr. and Mrs. Monroe" and "Ladies and Gentlemen's Guide to Modern English Usage" are very durable as comedy, as writing, and as insight.

Both Thurber's contributions to *Is Sex Necessary?* and his own first book, *The Owl in the Attic*, have limitations. If sometimes Homer nods, so also does Thurber. Although it is surprising and pleasant to find *Is Sex Necessary?* anticipating the New Morality or the Sexual Revolution of the 1960's, the book at times irritates because of its model. It illustrates the judgment that good parody requires a good original (burlesque, a lesser art form, thrives on bad models). Since psychologists and sociologists adore footnotes, the book is full of these and some are far too self-conscious. The reader suspects that Thurber and White went through and "did" the footnotes, and the result is much like a child who knows adults are watching him. The Fowler imitations do not copy Fowler, but rather, play a new melody on his theme. In the sex book, Thurber and White become slightly as tedious as the men they are ridiculing. Granted that any reader with taste prefers the parody to any original of the type, the parody still takes on some of the faults of the original. The "Guide," on the other hand, is a variation so well worked out that it confers pleasure in its own right independently of Fowler's original. Since sexologists and pet advice columnists are often intransigently stupid, or are often caught in the "box" of their own limitations, the comedy is not so free to discover what is new in the material. *Is Sex Necessary?* ridicules a poor original; the much more successful "Guide" invites thought on the comedy of language.

Despite its excellence, "Mr. and Mrs. Monroe" shows Thurber

trying one false direction which he abandoned immediately. He did not write ten sketches about Mr. and Mrs. Walter Mitty. Except for the character Thurber—and even he appears in various guises—Thurber never again re-uses characters. Although the subjects and dialogue in "Mr. and Mrs. Monroe" are in the familiar Thurber style, the very fact of the reappearance of characters causes the reader to expect development and change. The Monroes, however, are perfectly static. I suggested that Mr. Monroe seems older in later sketches; there is no evidence in the text that he develops, changes, or even grows older. In all his subsequent writing (with the possible exception of *The Years with Ross*, but I will have an explanation for that), we see Thurber's men and women intensely and completely, and then they are gone before we can ask questions about development or change. If Thurber's shade could speak to me, he would probably object that when I demand development, I am merely showing that I am caught in the conventions or expectations of the old-fashioned novel form. We know, in fact, that people seldom develop and change as they do in novels. Thurber is escaping, like many other twentieth-century artists, from conventions of time and development which falsify experience. Wallace Stevens views blackbirds in thirteen ways; Picasso sees his "Demoiselles d'Avignon" in multiple or mosaic perspective. If Thurber hoped in the Monroe sketches to get a multi-faceted perspective, he failed. We expect development. His later sketches and stories use collage or album effects (note his titles *The Thurber Album* and *The Thurber Carnival*). "Mr. and Mrs. Monroe" creates expectations which it does not satisfy; or, to put it another way, the form limits Thurber's comic freedom to get a greater mosaic or a greater complexity from experience.

Aside from these limitations—which are the same since they both show him extending what cannot be extended—the two books are astonishing performances for the beginning of a career. When they succeed, they illustrate the point that comedy at its best grapples with the human condition just as thoroughly as tragedy, satire, or romance. It may be that comedy is no more highly valued now than it was in Aristotle's time, but anyone who reads well recognizes the close relationship between the seriousness and the comedy in these two books. His subjects, to a surprising degree, will remain the same, but he will learn new skill and technique as he continues to try his subjects again and again. Even in these first two books, he increases his skill as a parodist. He discovers his themes when George Smith breaks the glass to solve the puzzle, when Mr. Monroe is frustrated by machines and social customs, when Mrs. Monroe's vitality gets her out of embarrassing situations, and when Thurber himself discovers the comedy of meaning. Later books modulate and develop the ideas — freedom, imprisonment by gadgets and systems, female vitality, illusive meaning — beyond all expectations of our fathers, but it is in the early books that he finds the themes and discovers their validity for the comic view of experience.

III

Comic Masks

Comedy is interested in Man as a social animal much more than it is interested in individual human beings. The ancient comic drama used masks for its characters, and although we find the idea of masks ludicrous, comedy, in a naturalistic way, actually preserves this convention. The people in modern comedy wear social masks; they are not, we know perfectly well, real people. They represent housewives, soldiers, suburbanites, bankers, politicians, or any other social role special enough and known enough to become a mask. The people we laugh at in comedy would be unbearable in life. Nor are we interested in them as moral agents; the moral consequences of their actions rarely bother or concern us. In one of Thurber's sketches an old man is rudely popped over the head with an ironing board, a whole city is misled by a stupid rumor, a distinguished doctor runs from a child on roller skates, and an army officer loses his courage when a child shouts at him. We look upon these strange actions (strange in our experience) with absolute aplomb and laugh; we are far removed from these cowards, parent strikers, victims of rumor. From our vantage point in the real world we look at these characters with the calculating and cold eye of a physicist disinterestedly eyeing the half-life of atomic structures. And the antic behavior provides pleasure. The ability to create these masks marks Thurber's comedy.

Thurber's *My Life and Hard Times* (1933) and *The Middle-Aged Man on the Flying Trapeze* (1935) illustrate comedy's delighted concern with man in society rather than with palpable human beings who might move us to tears. In 1931 Thurber began to publish his drawings in book form, and they make the same point. The drawings are, in a representative sense, crude. The simplest device separates men from women and all the men (and all the women) look exactly like all the others. They are objects engaged in their particular comic action or ritual. By the early 1930's Thurber had mastered, both in his writing and drawing, masks and rituals as simple and useful comic tools. Even when the subjects threaten to come close to us (and some do threaten our moral and emotional sensibilities) his saving comic skill pulls them away so that we can preserve a proper distance and keep on responding to comedy.

Comic Masks and the Self

My Life and Hard Times prints eight sketches written for the *New Yorker* (Chapter 7, "The Dog That Bit People" first appeared in the book) in 1931 and 1932 about life in Columbus, Ohio. In historical time, the events take place between 1908 and 1918. A "Preface to Life" and "A Note at the End" set the comic tone and give the book its unity. Within this comic scope Thurber uses his comic masks in that romantic enterprise, autobiography. Although for most of us the search for self, for identity, is serious and even agonizing, Thurber transforms it into a comic ritual. In the final essay the search for self and identity brings to memory the time when Thurber was trapped on a roller coaster:

> That trip, although it ended safely, made a lasting impression on me. It is not too much to say that it has flavored my life. It is the reason I shout in my sleep, refuse to ride on the elevated, keep jerking the emergency brake in cars other people are driving, have the sensation of flying like a bird when I first lie down, and in certain months can't keep anything on my stomach.

The Thurber character begins to do things—shout, refuse, jerk, fly, and vomit—that are either curiously inappropriate or else exactly what modern man suspects that he will do tomorrow, if he manages to get through today. Our own actual roller coaster produces pains, but when we see Thurber's response, it is as if we were watching over a fence, or through a telescope, to see someone else go through the actions.

In "University Days" the search for identity takes place in a biology lab, an appropriate place for our time. Again we have the thirsting soul, but this time, the discovery ends, as it so often does, right back where it began. For two terms the biology student has been trying to see plant cells; his professor has nearly given up hope until finally the student sees something and begins to make a quick sketch of what the microscope shows. The professor

> looked at my cell drawing. "What's that?" he demanded, with a hint of a squeal in his voice. "That's what I saw," I said. "You didn't, you didn't, you *did*n't!" he screamed, losing control of his temper instantly, and he bent over and squinted into the microscope. His head snapped up. "That's your eye!" he shouted. "You've fixed the lens so that it reflects! You've drawn your eye!"

As I have noted before, Thurber in both these examples finds comedy in what is quite serious business for many other writers. Some trivial event has changed our lives; the search for meaning in the universe has revealed only the self. In Wordsworth, Goethe, Stendhal or many of the other writers from the late eighteenth to the twentieth century, the subject is painful, sobering, and serious, but when the matter is displaced into a scene on a roller coaster (a common metaphor for life), the subject becomes comic. The screaming professor carries away any possible disappointment that the search of the universe has revealed only the self.

Thurber is using a device which is so patently a device and yet which is so natural that we accept it readily. The events occurred in 1914 and 1917 when people wore funny clothes, took funny biology courses with innocent and naive requirements, and rode, probably, very rickety roller coasters. When a romantic poet quests for the self, he makes us feel every anguished step. Thurber writes about another country where professors quiver a full six inches in either direction (a drawing goes with the text). This professor looks like Lionel Barrymore; if the memory of Lionel Barrymore is dim, then so much the better. Both the student and the professor are masks safely far enough away from us in time that we do not penetrate their surface; nor do we want to penetrate.

It is typical of comedy to ridicule its own methods, and ridicule is inevitable when the subject of the comedy is the self. In Molière's *Le Malade Imaginaire*, the main character rages against Molière for saying unkind things about doctors; in the original production Molière himself played the character. Thurber also makes fun of his need to objectify his events, his need to wear a mask. In the "Preface" Thurber writes, "Afraid of losing themselves in the larger flight of the two-volumed novel, or even the one-volume novel, [comic writers] stick to short accounts of their misadventures because they never get so deep into them but they feel they can get out." At the end of "The Day the Dam Broke" he reports that the city did not joke about the Great Run from the flood waters. To live through it was terrible; to learn about it twenty years later is possible. And again at the end of the book, Thurber returns to the subject for another laugh at our need to see events removed from present agonies or even the agonies in which the events might have occurred, before they can become comic rituals.

> The sharp edge of old reticences are softened in the autobiographer by the passing of time—a man does not pull the pillow over his head when he wakes in the morning because he suddenly remembers some awful thing that happened to him fifteen or twenty years ago, but the confusions and the panics of last year and the year before are too close for contentment. Until a man can quit talking loudly to himself in order to shout down the memories of blunderings and gropings, he is in no shape for the painstaking examination of distress and the careful ordering of event so necessary to a calm and balanced exposition of what, exactly, was the matter.

And, of course, the softening in the autobiographer has made the subjects funny; the calm and balanced exposition has shown what was the matter and what is comic.

In his "Preface" he goes one step further. Not only does he find comedy in his method and need for comic masks, but he *shows* how the almost Kafka-like terror of a landscape can be converted into comedy. Speaking of the comic autobiographer, Thurber writes,

> His gestures are the ludicrous reflexes of the maladjusted; his repose is the momentary inertia of the nonplussed. He pulls the blinds against the morning and creeps into smokey corners at night. He talks largely about small matters and smally about great affairs. His ears are shut to the ominous rumblings of the

dynasties of the world moving toward a cloudier chaos than ever
before, but he hears with an acute perception the startling sounds
that rabbits make twisting in the bushes along a country road at
night. . . . [He] keeps looking behind him as he walks along
darkening streets out of the fear that he is being softly followed
by little men padding along in single file, about a foot and a half
high, large-eyed, and whiskered.

His vision is like that of a surrealist. Or is it more like Eliot in
his "Preludes"? When a friend hears sounds which he says are
rabbits or reports being followed by midgets, we nervously reach
for a telephone or a strong drink. However, that man across the
street who slightly reminds me of surrealistic paintings or T. S.
Eliot (if I can pin him down to a name, I can control him) does
not frighten me at all. He is going through a routine, a ritual.
Thurber's ritualized language, "He talks largely about small matters and smally about great affairs," tells me not to care about
this social object moving in antic ways. The comic mask is firm
and sure.

My Life and Hard Times has a dog in nearly every sketch, and
includes Thurber's first sustained discussion of the creatures in
"The Dog That Bit People," written just for this book. Dogs are a
useful subject to Thurber because they permit him to see the foibles
of men as they are displaced in a dog. Muggs, the dog in the essay,
is testy, ill-mannered, and ferocious, and bites everyone that comes
within range. Even as a dog of experience he would be a difficult
subject for comedy. But he turns out to be an excellent comic mask;
he has taken on enough human traits to be recognizable but not
too many to be unbearable.

Behind its many social masks, autobiography charges right
into many supposedly non-comic ideas. Thurber writes about
death, burglary, entombment, suffocation, mothers sleeping in
the same room with their sons, mob scenes, machines with manic
minds of their own, the end of the world, fire in theaters, policemen
who can't handle their weapons, mad men walking in the night,
manic servants, nakedness, and the possibility of losing the Ohio
State—Illinois football game. We enjoy the comedy because it
gives us the opportunity to face such potentially horrendous events
knowing good and well that the events are so far removed from
us that we can only laugh at them.

We have been anesthetized because the characters involved are abstract mothers, cousins, doctors, lawyers, army officers, and even draftees. They are masks; they are not real people. Paradoxically, because these characters are masks we find them more pleasurable, the more frightening and bizarre their experience is. In "The Car We Had to Push" we learn about a family car, a Reo that after eight or ten years of indifferent service has finally been destroyed by a passing streetcar. The family mourns the loss extravagantly until Grandfather gets it into his head that someone has died. Nothing the family says can disabuse him of his idea; Grandfather attaches the name of his dead brother Zenas, who died of the Chestnut Blight after the Civil War, to the object of the family's mourning. To straighten out the old man, a friend is persuaded to dress up like Zenas, but Grandfather penetrates the hoax immediately. Had Grandfather indeed penetrated the family's behavior from the beginning? On the one hand he is just Grandfather, just the comic mask of an old man who has lost contact with the world of daily experience. He may be pitiable. On the other, we suspect that we have been tricked and that Grandfather has used his mask in order to make fun of the family's exaggerated reaction to the loss of the old car. We are told at the beginning that Grandfather does not know about automobiles, but after he penetrates the friend's disguise, he reminds the family that he had told them to buy a Pope-Toledo in the first place. Possibly the mask has been used to treat comically an important subject — American adulation of the automobile, draft dodgers, or the role of old men in the family. But at the same time, we are delighted when the Old Man pulls off his initial mask to reveal another, the mask of an alert, perceiving intelligence. Not only does Thurber employ the standard and necessary device of comic masks, but he uses it for further comic possibilities. He shifts the masks bewilderingly so that we do not know whether simply to laugh at the events or whether to look beyond for what Thurber may be telling us about our world. We are uncertain whether the comedy is pure, intended merely to provoke our laughter, or whether it is a mocking comment about our behavior.

Pure and Impure Comedy

My Life and Hard Times ends with Thurber regretting that he cannot be the wanderer, the "character out of Conrad, silent and inscrutable," who chases through the South Seas or the West Indies in search of further discovery. Once in Martinique, he tells us, he had a "quick, wild, and lovely moment when I decided I wouldn't get back on the ship. I did, though. And I found out that somebody had stolen the pants to my dinner jacket." The discovery is a prosaic anti-climax and it fails to provide the epiphany, the awakening, that the thirster after life demands. He cannot wander in the South Seas because he has to have his glasses changed or his teeth fixed. We cannot escape life for adventure. Thus, *My Life* has an artistic purity; it explores and exploits comic ideas. One might find a social comment in "The Day the Dam Broke" with its depiction of hysteria and mass paralysis of thought. An army officer joins the mob of citizens running away from the flood waters: "Used to quick decisions, trained to immediate obedience, the officer bounded off the porch and, running at full tilt, soon passed the child, bawling 'Go east!'" If nowhere else but in that sentence, one detects the same madness of society that caused countless men and women in our time, not to mention army officers, technicians, and engineers, all "trained to immediate obedience," to follow the hypnotic call of madmen just as the citizens of Columbus followed the officer shouting "Go east!" The reader makes the connection; Thurber never makes it. The comedy remains pure, an enjoyment of a social malaise that need not be compared to the horrors of the modern world.

Successfully handling a comic idea, Thurber sustains himself somewhere between working it out as pure comedy and gently slipping in a social statement. Many pieces in *The Middle-Aged Man on the Flying Trapeze* (1935) maintain this balance, but some come perilously close to objective statement. The first piece in the collection, "The Gentleman is Cold," plays with the comic idea inherent in modern man's encounter with the imponderable odds of his civilization: the problem of coping with overcoats. We are back, momentarily, in the world of Mr. Monroe, but the narrator is more acutely aware of his situation than Mr. Monroe, who is often either impervious to or only embarrassed by complexity. The essay has the typical three-part structure Thurber likes. In the first we learn how, because of the overcoat, Thurber lost his hat. In the second we discover his difficulties with doormen and porters who throw him in and out of the coat. Finally the overcoat causes social embarrassment in restaurants and in theaters and destroys his image of himself. At the climax Thurber tries to appear at ease in polite society after a hat-check boy has removed both the overcoat and his dinner jacket. He feels that

> red-faced fixed grin which no truly well-poised man-about-town ever permits himself to lapse into. I reached for my cigarettes, but I found that I had left them in a pocket of my overcoat, so in order to have something to do with my hands—for people were still staring and leering—I gracefully pulled a neatly folded handkerchief from the breast pocket of my dinner jacket, only to discover when I shook it out that it was a clean white silk sock.

The essay moves from private difficulties to public humiliation. One might say, "Damn a world that so embarrasses a man." One might read it as a ridicule of social habits, an *impure* comedy of errors.

Thurber's exact but unobtrusive language preserves the purity of the comedy. The italicized words in the following paragraph, the opening one, qualify the experience so that ordinary things are presented to the mind in an unusual aspect.

> In the first *chill* days of November it was the subject of sharp and rather *nasty* comment on the part of my friends and colleagues that I went about the *draughty* streets of town without a hat or overcoat. Once even a stranger who passed me in the street *snarled*, "Put on your hat and coat!" It seemed to *annoy* people. They began to *insinuate* under their breath, and even come right out and say, that I was simply trying to look *strange* and *different* to attract attention.

The "*smirking* remarks and *mean* innuendos" finally force him to wear an overcoat, but he refuses to buy another hat, for the view he gets of himself in hat shop mirrors makes him "look like a slightly ill professor of botany who is also lost." The neat, precise words constantly qualify the situation. They become a dance, a ritual, almost a mask, existing in an antic comic world of their own, and thus the words turn us back to the comic goal of exploiting the idea.

"The Departure of Emma Inch," the second sketch, uses a purely comic idea but also flirts with Thurber's perennial interest in the meaning of meaning in a complicated society. Emma is one

of that long line of Thurber servants who do not have the brain
to cope with ordinary experience. They muffle through life, driving
Thurber crazy and never satisfying themselves. They stand in contrast to the dogs; for though the dogs do not understand either,
they at least have a native animal instinct to guide them. Emma
Inch is trampled under. She is frightened of automobiles, terrified
by ships, and shocked by telephones. She thinks that her dog talks
and sings. We see her finally setting out to walk from the eastern
end of Massachusetts to New York carrying her neurotic dog.
She is a "Man with a Hoe" in comic terms. She smiles only once:
at the end, when she finally disengages herself from the ship and
all that it represents of organized life. She is kin to Thurber's
grandmother who screwed light bulbs into empty sockets to keep
the electricity from leaking all over the house, or Thurber's mother
who warned her sons not to drive the car without gasoline because
"it fried the valves, or something." Thurber's relatives, however,
have vitality; their imperfect report of experience does not matter
since they have an order of their own. Poor Emma Inch is victimized
by everything including her dog. Her inability to comprehend is
funny in the tradition of that familiar comic type, the country
bumpkin, yet the world of ships, telephones, and automobiles
must take some responsibility for her terrible plight. The reader
is caught between the desire to laugh and his recognition of injustice.

Several of Thurber's stories in *The Middle-Aged Man on the
Flying Trapeze* tell us about the ineffectual Thurber man. He is
not quite as pitiable as Emma Inch, but the twinge of recognition
is there. We enjoy a lover in a Chaplin comedy, according to Al
Capp, chiefly because no matter how bad we are as lovers, we are
not that bad. So also with Thurber's men. We may lack acuteness
or fail in insight as drivers, husbands, or fathers (social masks all)
but we are not quite that bad; and yet we are nearly that bad.
Consider Mr. Pendly who "mistook a pond for a new concrete road
and turned off onto it. . . . You can't drive toward a body of water
thinking it's made of concrete without having your grip on your-
self permanently loosened." Mr. Bentley, in a sketch called "The
Indian Sign," has a daughter whom his wife has insisted upon
naming Cora after some ancestor. The family story that an early
American Cora "was more than a match for nineteen males affected

Henry Bentley dismally." Or, for another example, in "The Private Life of Mr. Bidwell," the word *goop*, a word his wife applies to him when she discovers him holding his breath, annoys Bidwell. It also spurs him on to continue and expand the habit: he takes to holding his breath more and more frequently, at parties, and at home. His wife is driven to distraction and, finally, to divorce. He is last seen walking down a road "trying to see how many steps he could take without opening his eyes." Poor Charlie Deshler in "The Curb in the Sky," unwittingly marries a woman who always corrects his stories. There is no escape. He ends up in a madhouse recounting a dream to a visitor—but his bright-eyed wife is sitting devotedly by his bedside and she now corrects his account of his own dream. Mr. Preble, in "Mr. Preble Gets Rid of His Wife," agrees to act on his stenographer's flippant response that, yes, they should run off together. But first he must murder his wife and bury her in the cellar. The wife understands poor Preble too well; she goes along to the cellar and evaluates his plans. These skeletal descriptions might lead one to suppose that the stories are only comic because of Thurber's language or because of their preposterous situations. In each case, however, the surge of felt life at the end marks a triumph for the poor befuddled characters and provides the reader with a comic release.

"Mr. Pendly and the Poindexter" is an excellent illustration of the man whose seeming defeat is still comic (the story is an early version of "The Secret Life of Walter Mitty"). Shopping with his wife for a car, Pendly is victimized by his wife's superior knowledge of things mechanical. The wife, a salesman, and a very superior mechanic, however, cannot open the trunk on a Poindexter that the Pendlys are considering. They ignore Pendly; he stands off to one side looking "like a slightly ill professor of botany who is also lost," as Thurber had described himself earlier. However, in his simple directness, Pendly discovers a way to open the trunk. He does not reveal his discovery. The world of mechanism goes grinding on—the wife, the salesman, and the mechanic do not notice. But Pendly knows and that seems enough. Mr. Bidwell—who held his breath and walked with eyes closed—defeated his wife and won the privilege of doing what he wanted to do. The madness of Charlie Deshler is the only victory possible over a woman who has the incorrigible habit of correcting stories. Preble, even with his wife's exposure of his murder schemes, is still hurrying on with his plan like a clockwork mannequin.

In every case, the comedy stems from the fact that the world is destroying a man. The stories are not satires, mordantly attacking mechanical systems or failures of vision. They are very comic because they run us through the potential disasters of life but find—in the very instant of social and personal defeat—some way for the comic release of pure laughter. Pendly discovers how to open the trunk lid; Emma Inch smiles for the first time in her life when she escapes from the ferry to Martha's Vineyard and starts her walk back to New York with her neurotic dog.

The critic Wylie Sypher says that "The ambivalence of comedy reappears in its social meanings, for comedy is both hatred and revel, rebellion and defense, attack, and escape. . .revolutionary and conservative, . . .both sympathy and persecution." Sypher means, I believe, that the masks of comedy cover greater ranges of material than most of us would ordinarily think. Further, behind the mask, the comic writer can move a great deal more easily. Thurber's comic language is a kind of mask, since the minute we catch its urbane, distracted tone we are ready to allow the characters described in that language to hunt for boxes to hide in or for not so lonely places to talk. The parodies of Cain, Stein, Galsworthy and others give Thurber the room to attack and admire at the same time. The menaced man is another of these masks. Mr. Pendly hates his inferiority to the auto mechanic, the salesman, and his wife, but he revels in his victory when he opens the trunk. His refusal to tell is a kind of reveling and counter-attack against his oppressors.

At the end of "A Preface to Dogs," another story in *The Middle-Aged Man*, a daughter dog suddenly recognizes her mother just as the two begin to hunt a fat woodchuck. Already the sketch has compared human parents unfavorably to dog parents: dog parents forget their children, a much more healthy attitude than the human one. For a moment the daughter recognizes her mother and asks her parent to look at her ear, a long, floppy ear apt to pick up a tick or a burr.

> Instantly the other dog bristled and growled. "I'm not your mother," she said. "I'm a woodchuck hunter." The daughter grinned.

"Well," she said, just to show there were no hard feelings, "that's not my ear, it's a motorman's glove."

The dogs are a mask behind which Thurber can speak more fully and more pleasingly than Philip Wylie could ever speak on the subject of momism in his *A Generation of Vipers*. In writing the sketch Thurber thought neither of momism nor of the purity or impurity of his comedy. It is simply the method and habit of comedy to use these masks, and the most satisfactory comedy will balance its one impulse to indulge in complete play against another impulse to indulge in complete statement. The appreciative reader of Thurber's comedy is he who can detect this ambivalence or balance in the social meanings or the social masks which comedy adopts. Some critics of comedy prefer to emphasize the statement and test Thurber's comedy by its range of statement, by how much he attacks Galsworthy's idiocy or Emma Inch's stupidity. Another critic (and I think this is the healthier impulse) prefers to see the antic pleasure of the comedy. The point here is that not only are both necessary but that the extension of one is apt to be an extension of the other. Thus a new mask — say, the imitation of James in "Something to Say" — opens further possibilities for statement.

Comedy and Human Emotions

Comedy's worst enemy is sentimental identification with the comic characters. We laugh at a man in a top hat who slips on a banana peel and takes a pratfall. We would not laugh if we knew he was on his way to a theater to make one last desperate effort to win a five dollar talent prize to pay his dying mother's hospital bill. Henri Bergson claims that the distinguishing characteristic of comedy is the fact that it must fall "on the surface of a soul that is thoroughly calm and unruffled." He goes on to say that if we "Look upon life as a disinterested spectator, [then] many a drama will turn into a comedy." Comedy "demands something like a momentary anesthesia of the heart. Its appeal is to intelligence, pure and simple." (See *Works Consulted*) His ideas are exactly illustrated in Thurber's story of the origin of the famous "Touche!" cartoon. Carl Rose submitted the original drawing of a fencer slashing off his opponent's head. Harold Ross, the *New Yorker* editor, thought the original cartoon was too bloody and gruesome, but he gave the idea to Thurber because "Thurber's people have no blood. You can put their heads back on and they're as good as new." The comic method enables us to see the idea and not be distracted by the blood.

It would seem, therefore, that an excellent comic artist is ever going to attempt new subjects which he can handle by the power of his established comic method. Thurber establishes the right of his "pure" comedy to consider painful subjects like Emma Inch and still make them comic. To use Bergson's words, his comedy anesthetizes us to accept the idea of a fencer trying too hard and slashing off the head of his opponent, but he still responds with the ritual of fencing and pronounces the familiar word. Another obvious example is a sketch entitled "If Grant Had Been Drinking at Appomattox." Grant, according to common knowledge, liked his bottle. Thurber imagines the scene that might have occurred if he had been drunk at the time of Lee's surrender. In Thurber's version, Grant gives his sword to Lee and repeats all of the familiar military ritual just as the fencer repeats "Touche!" The admirable quality of Thurber's comedy is that he constantly expands his material to include new rituals. He makes some admirable criticism of James M. Cain, Galsworthy, a whole school of inscrutable British short story writers, or an obvious target like Miss Gertrude Stein. The comic form enables him to strip away the emotions from these subjects (one could be passionately committed to the vision of Cain or Stein) and see, with our intelligence, the aspect of their writing that is comic. What is laughable about Grant's drinking or a fencer's behavior is found in the literary habits of the writers that Thurber uses for his subjects. Our soul is made calm and unruffled so that we can understand Stein's maddeningly ellip- tical and enigmatic vision or Cain's crudities as pure idea. Our intelligence is brought into play.

Thurber is superior in finding surprising new ways to bring intelligence into play. The two final pieces in *The Middle-Aged Man* front Prufrock-like characters with what might be really terrible situations. In both cases we detect the drama of lonely, even terrified, men, but we see the men disinterestedly, without judging their situations. We impose no emotional, ethical, moral, religious, or political judgment on them. In the first of these two pieces, "One is a Wanderer," a lonely man on a Saturday night tries to find some way to occupy his time: "Two is company," he says, "four is a party, three is a crowd. One is a wanderer." The piece is comic because we anesthetize our hearts to this man going

>...through certain half-deserted streets
>The muttering retreats
>Of restless nights.

The narrator walks on Broadway, goes to his office, sits in a bar. He explains to the bartender, "But you see, George, I am an analyzer. I am also a rememberer. I have a pocketful of old used years. You put all those things together and they sit in a lobby getting silly and old." The terrible situation is pathetic but it is also comic because the reader thinks, inappropriately, of Hamlet or Prufrock or even the fencer continuing his ritual. The story, of course, is not humorous. No one laughs out loud. Further the lonely man lacks Bidwell's mad energy that sends him walking with his eyes closed or even the energy of Charlie Deshler's retreat to his madhouse. The Wanderer is a sad man repeating a sad ritual.

In the final piece in *The Middle-Aged Man*, "A Box to Hide In," a man seeks a large box. He explains to an incredulous but unfeeling grocer that "It's a form of escape, . . .hiding in a box. It circumscribes your worries and the range of your anguish. You can't see people, either." He asks his cleaning lady ("She's awful but she has a big heart, which makes it worse") if she knows of a box, and he works out a phantasy in which her discovery of him causes a heart attack and death. The piece ends with the narrator, unsatisfied, still hunting for a box with all the manic indirection of a man conducting an orchestra without any musicians. There's no blood, just the men caught in their quirk of loneliness. In another piece, "The Remarkable Case of Mr. Bruhl," a perfectly ordinary, middle-class man is mistaken for a well-known criminal. A childhood accident has left him with a scar similar to that of the criminal and identification with the criminal finally causes Mr. Bruhl to act the life that people insist that he should lead. He dies in a country hotel, refuses to tell the police who shot him, and mutters "Cop!" when they press him for an explanation. He is lured to his terrible death by a practical joker who thought the resemblance funny. Again the quirk of behavior is sufficient to anesthetize the reader

so that he can see the comic idea of a respectable citizen acting
as if he were a criminal even up to his moment of death. We know
that Mr. Bruhl has seen too many movies and read too many newspapers just as the other two men, wandering and alone, have
read too much romantic poetry. But still, in all the laughter, there
is a little to hurt.

Two others of his characters in *The Middle-Aged Man* act out
exceptional roles in society; each man is a potential hero to his
society but somehow gets locked in his role so fixedly that his
drama becomes a comedy. The point of these stories is not the
loneliness and isolation of ordinary man, but the absurd way in
which our complex society celebrates what it conceives of as genius.
In "Something to Say," a fatuous narrator describes the last hectic
days and death of his friend, Elliot Vereker, a self-proclaimed
genius. The narrator and his friends have believed passionately
in Vereker, yet it is his eccentric, antic, and outrageous behavior
rather than anything he has actually done that has convinced
them of his talent. He was "the most burning genius we had ever
been privileged to know," the narrator tells us. But he also mentions that when his friends had collected a fund to send Vereker
to Europe to write, "His entire output, I had discovered, consisted
of only twenty or thirty pages, most of them bearing the round
stain of liquor glasses; one page was the beginning of a play done
more or less in the style of Gertrude Stein. It seemed to me as
brilliant as anything of its kind." Although Vereker has supposedly
been working on a novel, "Sue You Have Seen," nobody has in
fact seen it. If we believe the narrator, Vereker was a lion stunted
by his civilization. But every new revelation of Vereker's life by
the narrator deepens the reader's suspicion that Vereker was
uproariously living up to his friends' notions of how a genius
should act. Thus the story is a savage attack on the cheapening
of the idea of genius in the twentieth century. A painful subject
has been transformed into a subject for laughter, especially for
the reader who recognizes "Something to Say" as an imitation
(certainly not a parody) of Henry James's story, "The Death of
a Lion."

The James story, a marvelous illustration of the Jamesian
range of tone, also describes a writer consumed by his public,
and both stories are narrated by a somewhat dim-witted hack

convinced of the essential genius of his subject. In the James story, the hero, Neil Paraday, has written a long prospectus of a new fiction which astounds the narrator, but which Paraday's admirers mislay. They have not read beyond page fifteen of his most recent fiction, just as Vereker's admirers have never seen anything of his work. James's story is just as ambiguous in tone as Thurber's, though Neil Paraday is clearly the victim. In James's story the creative mind is victimized by princesses and ladies of fashion; in Thurber's story, most significantly, Vereker's mind is as much victimized by his own myth — for he must behave in his antic fashion to prove his genius to his friends — as by his public.* Quite clearly Vereker is an ass; and so is the narrator who is taken in by Vereker's claims. But of the two, Vereker seems a shade more admirable. Our society demands genius but does not know how to tell a true one from a fraud. Vereker pays us a lesson in his mad and extravagant imitation of "genius," and gives us what we want. He has learned his lines from newspapers, journals, and books; he has whored to his public and his public has willingly paid him fifteen hundred dollars for the pleasure. He is a monster, but he is a monster created by a society that confuses a vague quality marked by eccentricity, intuitive judgment, carelessness and· a certain disdain for the rights of others with the genuine attributes of genius.

The second story, also on the masks of genius, is another imitation of a popular form. "The Greatest Man in the World," is modeled on the popular journalistic reports on the technological hero of our time. Vereker is the old-fashioned hero of a novel-reading civilization; Jack ("Pal") Smurch is the hero of the brave

---

*Thurber's name for the hero in "Something to Say," Elliot Vereker, comes directly from Hugh Vereker, the novelist with the secret in his fiction, in James's story, "The Figure in the Carpet." Thurber likes James's title phrase and uses it in "A Final Note on Chanda Bell" (*Thurber Country*), a story about a female Hugh Vereker. Another Jamesian character, Leolin Fane, is nearly as frightening as Elliot. Remembering Thurber's everlasting fondness for word games, I can't help but notice that the letters in *Leolin* are, except for the final *t* and *n*, the same as in Elliot. Leolin, the social flower son of a mother who writes high society novels, will never write a novel although his foolish mother believes that he has the necessary genius and experience, and that she has properly taught him his craft. Her attitude toward Leolin, indulgent respect and hope, is much like the attitude of Elliot Vereker's friends in Thurber's story. Leolin appears in a story entitled "Greville Fane," the pseudonym his mother uses to sign her pot-boilers. I am grateful to Robert Gale for leading me through the intricacies of Jamesian short fiction.

new world. The sketch is internally dated as a report written in 1940 about an event in 1937, but the sketch appears in a book published in 1935 and Robert Morsberger dates the original publication of the story as 1931, four years after Charles Lindbergh's celebrated trans-Atlantic flight. "Pal" Smurch clamps the "long-distance refuelling device of a crazy schoolmaster" to a rickety airplane and flies the plane around the world non-stop. The public is as ready to adulate him for his courage and his success as Elliot Vereker's public was ready for him. Jack Smurch, however, has a reformatory record; "the story of his life cannot be printed"; Jack has no concept of the "ethics and behavior of heroism." He blatantly seeks monetary rewards; he sits down when the President is brought in to meet him. He is a ghastly representative of western technological civilization, but he has that rare commodity, physical stamina.

The comedy is intentionally ambiguous. Does it cut against the Pal Smurches in the world, the men who can act but have no conception of an ideal of action? Or against the newspapermen who, discovering that their story is not fit to print, fabricate a better one to feed the masses? Finally a secretary to the Mayor of New York pushes Smurch out of an open window nine stories above the street: an Associated Press editor arranges the funerary details:

> Crisply he ordered certain men to leave, others to stay; quickly he outlined a story which all the papers were to agree on, sent two men to the street to handle that end of the tragedy, commanded a Senator to sob, and two Congressmen to go to pieces nervously. In a word, he skillfully set the stage for the gigantic task that was to follow, the task of breaking to a grief-stricken world the sad story of the untimely, accidental death of its most illustrious and spectacular figure.

The story is comic and horrible. It tests the ability of a civilization to create its heroes. Is it enough to have the stamina to fly around the world? Is it enough to claim loudly, as Elliot Vereker does, that "Achievement is the fool's gold of idiots"? Should we read the comedy in relation to a society that has such shoddy public values as "money" and a public image that Smurch wanted? Is the comedy directed against the newspapers that must invent strange gods? After the accidental death, a public funeral is held and "At a given hour there were two minutes of silence throughout the nation." Agents of the Department of Justice have been sent to a shack restaurant in Iowa to make sure of Smurch's mother:

> One of them was especially assigned to stand grimly in the doorway of a little shack restaurant on the edge of the tourist's camping ground just outside the town. There, under his stern scrutiny, Mrs. Emma Smurch bowed her head above two hamburger steaks sizzling on her grill — bowed her head and turned away, so that the Secret Service man could not see the twisted, strangely familiar, leer on her lips.

Comedy cannot go much further (a) into the area of social affairs, (b) into the conflict of its own desire to remain pure and its desire to comment on life, and (c) into forcing us to hold our emotions in abeyance so that we can perceive, with an anesthetized heart, a comic action. Without speaking of value directly, Thurber makes his reader think of value. He finds new material for comic ritual.

Comedy's instinct is to consider man in society and to ignore feeling about characters; it remains poised between the desire to cudgel society for its vices and the desire to ignore social behavior so as to concentrate on the laughter in a situation. The writer of comedy takes more and more into his comic world, and after the laughter, a comic story may linger in the mind to reverberate against the reader's experience.

Emma Inch, Grandfather, Elliot Vereker, Pal Smurch, and the sad, lonely, unnamed men who wander the streets of the city are comic masks totally representing a comic idea. It is the skill of comedy to strip away from personalities all the human dross which might engage emotions so that the comedy can concentrate on laughter. By placing his action in the distant world of Columbus, Ohio, between 1908 and 1913 Thurber encourages the reader to see simply and starkly these men and women without blood in them. We can bear them in that distant world and we can laugh at them. They are figures in a ritual, but it is a ritual that is ever expanding to include new aspects of the human experience. I turn now to another aspect of that ritual, its ending.

IV

The Comic Ending

Ask any man on the street what comedy is and he will say that it is a funny play with a happy ending. In addition to the basic element of laughter, comedies go on until everyone gets married and lives happily ever after. If we rule out Thurber's fairy tales, only one of his creations has the conventional ending, the play he wrote with Elliott Nugent, *The Male Animal*. Even the play, however, in typical resistance to neat categories, cannot be described by a simple formula. The story and the characters are familiar Thurber interests, and the theatrical shaping, I suspect, comes from Nugent, who was a professional theater man in the best sense of those words. However Thurber did write theatrical productions for theater groups at Ohio State in the early 1920's, and he was, to judge from his constant interest in the theater, always a theater buff. His one play is conventional in structure, especially when contrasted to the innovation in the essays. The Broadway theater, for good and obvious reasons, must be more conventional than an essay that fills two pages of a weekly magazine. Further, by comparing the way that the play works with the way that the essays work, I find, most surprisingly, that Thurber discovered and exploited a new comic mask. Comic characters are stock figures; they always have been and they always will be. Every modern writer uses familiar types that were probably old when Aristophanes—who is, after all, only the oldest known practitioner of what was already a very sophisticated art—used them.

Thurber's new comic type does not appear in *The Male Animal*; the new type does appear in the collection of essays *Let Your Mind Alone*. Thurber's special way with comic endings and his astonishing creative act of developing a new comic mask become clear when the play is used as a ground design to throw into relief the structure of the essays. I am willing to praise the play for its own sake; it shows Thurber working toward the genuinely satisfactory endings of *The Thurber Album* and *The Years with Ross*. The play is also useful in explaining the success of a series of drawings entitled *The Last Flower.*

The Struggle in Thurber's Comedy

Every comedy, when stripped down to its basic essentials, involves only two characters: on one side a young hero (a New King) representing life and freedom and on the other an old man (the Old King) who threatens the hero. The old man represents authority, order, repression, and since he is frequently a liar or a pretender, he is known by the technical name of *impostor*. When he is overthrown, the hero is awarded a prize, a young lady, and the marriage that ends the comedy signifies the birth of a new society that the young hero has given us a glimpse of. Lesser characters in the drama exist only to heighten the distinction between the hero and the impostor or to bring the struggle to a successful victory for the young man.

Critics and anthropologists have noted over and over again that sophisticated modern comedy repeats a pattern or structure of the primitive seasonal rite that I have just described. Ancient man enacted the ritual of the Old King, associated with the sins and errors of his community during the winter, and a New King, representing the new hopes for life, fertility, and the community's desires for the coming summer. The most ancient comedies are clearly fertility rites, celebrating the god of fertility; they were performed in the spring of the year and they represent mankind's constant hope for rebirth and eternal life. They celebrate the male principle embodied in the Greek god, Phales, who appears in the marriage hymn, the *Comos*, which ends all of ancient Greek comedy (and gives us our word *comedy*). In a quite genuine sense, those plays are plays too about the male animal.

This pattern of the death of winter and the birth of summer

helps us see what is happening in Thurber's comedy, a comedy
written for a civilization that thinks of spring as a season of daf-
fodils and winter as a season when the theater is active and the
streets are full of slush. Thurber's comedy is both very much like
the ancient ritual and very different. Even his essays, which do
not seem dramatic in the ordinary sense of the term, resemble the
ancient form. Because his comedies repeat the ancient ritual, they
truly impinge on our humanity and enable us to re-enact the basic
struggles of civilization. Civilization is the game that we play
to act out perennial and serious questions in a distant and removed
world of art forms so that we can understand, see, and even appreciate the experience that most of us are too busy to taste and savor.
I must compare Thurber's comedy—and again the play is the
clearest example for comparison—with this primary human drama
of rebirth in order to demonstrate the great seriousness of his
comedy. *The Male Animal* concerns primitive and primary qualities
of our character. The play is not just a story about an English
professor who insists on reading a letter to undergraduates at
a large midwestern university; the play says it concerns the need
and right of expression against repressive, stupid, powerful forces
which will, if they can, kill American society. By comparing the
play to the ancient ritual, I am showing how complicated and
interesting this well-constructed play is. By comparing the essays
to this play, I am showing how much more Thurber accomplishes
in the little room of his essays.

A modern vulgarity says that everything is really simple. Comparisons and distinctions, this barbarism suggests, are really unnecessary. "We exist independent of our past. We feel and that
is enough. We have our values and only our values are relevant."
Thurber attacks just such simplicity in "Soapland," a long analysis
of radio drama in *The Beast in Me.* Popular newspapers and magazines headline simple, naive, childish explanations of good, evil,
and comedy. We are corrupted and cheapened when we give in
to such easy explanations. The play that Thurber and Nugent
wrote is a complicated examination of issues that man has been
concerned with as far back as our records go. It so happens that
Aristophanes and the Greek theater are our most complete and
ancient record, and it so happens that scholars and critics have
analyzed the forces in that society with clarity and energy. We

say that we should use our past to understand our present; it behooves us to follow our shibboleths. Seeing Thurber's play in conjunction with the habits of a rich, ancient tradition enriches and deepens our appreciation of what Thurber does. He recreates his civilization. He is speaking about a special phenomenon, the university witch-hunts in the 1930's, but he speaks in a form that connects the accidents and stupidities of 1939 with, to use an old-fashioned phrase, universal truths.

It would be foolish, of course, to argue that a writer in the mid-twentieth century exactly imitates spring festivities in Athens, but modern man in his modes of laughter expresses the same human impulse that made primitive man celebrate rites of spring. We do not think of an Old Year as dead (just an old man on New Year's cards), nor do we prepare rituals to insure that women will be fertile, fields produce grain and wine, or weather be benign. Intellectual systems, naked monetary power, formidable women, and high speed automobiles threaten us. Our comedy, therefore, celebrates man's indomitable nature that will not be repressed by vulgar ideologists, psychologists, indignant university trustees, bossy wives, or rampaging machines. The model or pattern of comedy is the same; the material fleshing out the model differs greatly. I am sure Thurber never knew the model of comedy; I have no evidence that he ever read Aristophanes or modern academic critics. If he had, he would have found an excellent subject for comedy. Thurber and Nugent did have the instinctive knowledge of the artist, the felt understanding of the same currents, because they worked in theaters. The model of the ancient comedy helps Thurber's readers to see how the ancient *Comos* becomes a celebration of our agonies made joyful by a new Male Animal. Thurber wrote to show how life triumphs over forces which make it a mere formula. For the nonce, however, the formula of comedy will be useful as a contrast to see how Thurber's endings once more vary a familiar habit. He makes what might be old and familiar seem bright and new. Once we see the formula, we can discover how he goes beyond it.

In *The Male Animal* an Old King of physical and monetary power, allied with conservative political judgments, tries to destroy a New King of intelligence and felt understanding. The New King is Tommy Turner, professor of English literature and composition at a large, midwestern state university. His opposition, the Old King, is the board of trustees and the alumni who fear that Turner will upset the *status quo*. He might, heaven forfend, put some ideas into the heads of his students. Turner champions free examination of human experience: the trustees and alumni want to make sure that the faculty remains docile, that the football team wins, and that the young are not damaged by ideas. The locus of this opposition is the character of Joe Ferguson, a Pittsburgh steel executive, ex-football player, ex-rival and new rival for the professor's wife. Joe, a close friend of the trustee in the play, represents the trustee point of view. He is bourgeois and respectable; he thinks only in the largest and most readily available clichés; he has physical strength, assured manners, and money. He not only tries to persuade the professor to accept the trustee point of view, but he also threatens to take the professor's wife. The professor, with everything against him except the audience's sympathy, defeats the threat and, at the end of the play, defies Joe Ferguson and his power. He reads, or he will read, to his classes the letter written by Bartolomeo Vanzetti. By that act, he regains the respect and, we believe, the love of his wife. By that act, a new society will be born. Even if he is fired—and he may well be—he will now live like a man. The play celebrates and praises the principle that Tommy Turner acts upon.

If we are close to the play, we see a modern problem. If we stand back from the play—as if we were standing at one end of a gallery to look at a painting at the opposite end—we see that the design is traditional and very familiar. Tommy Turner is the New King, and he wears the stock mask (as in a Greek play) of the life-giving, creative force in society. Because he decides to read the letter, the board of trustees will fire him. If he does not thus assert his manhood, he will lose his wife to Jumping Joe Ferguson. The life-force that he represents is the life of liberal intelligence that he defends in his speech:

> Don't you see this isn't about Vanzetti. This is about us! If I
> can't read this letter today, tomorrow none of us will be able to
> teach anything except what Mr. Keller [the trustee] here and
> the Legislature permit us to teach. Can't you see what this leads
> to—what it has led to in other places? We're holding the last

fortress of free thought, and if we surrender to prejudice and
dictation, we're cowards.

Spring is in the air (although the play takes place in autumn),
and the voice of the turtle is heard throughout the land. The old
forces of prejudice, settled law and order, and physical repression
have been routed. When Turner recovers the principle of action,
he defeats Joe Ferguson and the trustee who wanted to prevent
him from taking any action. Even Dr. Damon, Turner's department chairman, had counselled quietness, appeasement. The professor's intelligence replaces the simple vitality of the ancient
play and the ancient fertility rite; it is his intelligence rather than
the grotesque phallus of the Greek play, that is the male principle
here. We have one more example of the delight man takes in his
mental gifts and mental vitality; Turner triumphs over the obstacles of commercial civilization because his mind and courage
are superior.

When Turner acts to read the letter, he puts Joe Ferguson to
rout. Joe goes back to his Pittsburgh wife, and we know that he
is a defeated man (but not so badly defeated that we sympathize
with him). Turner's marriage will be resumed because Turner is
now a Male Animal. Ferguson turns out to be a liar or (in the more
technical term) an impostor. What he believes, his bourgeois explanation, is proved to be a lie. Thus the term *impostor* is not only
historically justified—because the ancient comedy had such false
seducers—but justified by the behavior before us.

The first ten sketches in *Let Your Mind Alone* have exactly
the same pattern of life forces of intelligence triumphing over
dead liars or impostors. What might surprise the reader is the fact
that the impostors, the Joe Fergusons, of these sketches are the
authors of self-help books which brim with advice on how to exploit the mind. The self-help authors, at first glance, would seem
to be the New King who will overthrow old prejudice, but they
are quickly revealed as deader than dead. The titles of their books
illustrate how they lie: *Streamline Your Mind, Unmasking Our
Minds, How to Worry Successfully, Wake Up and Live*, and *Be
Glad You're Neurotic*. Thurber, by the way, reports actuality; he
is not inventing. These impostors, the authors of such works,
are old, restraining, complacent, and sterile. If a man followed
their advice, he would be dead as a human being. They reduce

palpable experience to the most vulgar of charades. When the hero, the speaker in each sketch, exposes the actual triteness and uselessness of their advice, the reader feels the new spring of life, the male principle, just as he feels joy when Turner marches off to read Vanzetti's letter.

Let Your Mind Alone delights the reader with a second contest. In these sketches, Thurber, in the way familiar to comedy, complicates his pattern. He obscures his method. Our expectations are confounded. We understand the main contest between the narrator and the inspirational writers, but to illustrate the error of the inspirationalists, the narrator tells stories in which heroes are clobbered and destroyed. The reader is pulled two ways at once, toward a comic release and toward a painful realization. The second sketch in the book, "Destructive Forces in Life," illustrates the double contest. The narrator is quarrelling with "the learned Mr. David Seabury, author of 'What Makes Us Seem So Queer,' 'Unmasking Our Minds,' 'Keep Your Wits,' 'Growing Into Life,' and 'How to Worry Successfully'": according to the narrator Seabury's choice of problems for illustration is in "the main unimaginative and pedestrian." Not so Thurber's mind. The full sketch has Thurber's three-part structure: (1) the illustration provided by the story of Frank Fulsome who speaks cruelly to his wife because he hates his boss; (2) the counter-illustration of Bert Scursey who cannot resist playing tricks on the telephone; and (3) further difficulties on the telephone that the authors of inspirational books have not considered. Thurber fully develops the Scursey interlude, but with the others the reader is left to fill in the details himself on the principle that if heard melodies are sweet, unheard melodies are sweeter (and untold stories funnier). To prove that Seabury, the psychologist who thinks he knows all the answers, is unimaginative, the narrator relates the case of Scursey who masquerades as a "Colored Woman Who Has Not Organized Her Life." We know, therefore, that he is a liar and impostor. Scursey's opponent is Harry Connor, a man trying to keep some vestige of sense and order in his life. At the end of the sketch, Scursey has so undone poor Harry Conner that he moves out of his apartment, out of New York City, and takes "a less important position" in Oregon, a sea coast of Bohemia where life is more human since Scursey is not there.

Which side of the contest between Scursey and Conner do we follow with sympathy? Scursey is the aggressor, like the football player, who should be routed, but Scursey wins and sends Conner to exile in Oregon! The narrator's major point—life cannot be reduced to the psychologist's pattern—supports Scursey's cruel attack, and within the comic structure there is another picture with the bitter-turning thought of exile. Harry Conner is defeated, but in his defeat he asserts his will. Because he ultimately escapes from Scursey, we feel a surge of vitality even in the midst of his defeat. Exile is bitter, but in Oregon a man may live.

In *The Male Animal* and in the first sketches of *Let Your Mind Alone* Thurber recasts the old contest between the old forces and the younger, life-giving, victorious men. In these early essays, the victor is usually carrying a scar. Tommy Turner's victory is not quite sure, but he has sent Joe Ferguson back to Pittsburgh. Harry Conner, however, only escapes from Bert Scursey. The struggle is one of conservative power and authority against liberal freedom. I will discuss this struggle again. It is enough to say here that the two parts of the contest have dramatic (active, visible) representation in Thurber's one play and in the sketches, and the ending marks some kind of triumph for a character who acts for a better, freer and more liberal world.

The Stock Masks in the Contest

Comedy employs four distinct types of characters. Two types (or masks) are necessary to the action and the other two intensify or focus the comedy. For the action we need the mask of the *eiron*, the winner of the comic struggle, and the boasting impostor who tries to thwart the hero so that he himself can carry off the prize.

The word *hero* is not accurate since often victors in comic struggles lack heroic qualities. As often as not they are rascals. *Eiron* is a neutral word without the familiar associations of the word *hero*. If the *eiron* is not young, he will suddenly become young at the end of the play. In the Greek comedy, he frequently starts as an old man who is magically transformed into a young bridegroom at the end of the play. Robert Morsberger in his book *James Thurber* objects that Tommy Turner is an "unrealistic" representation of a college professor because he is too young to be promoted to a full professor and publication in the *Atlantic*

Monthly and *Harper's* does not ordinarily win promotion for American academics. A Broadway audience would hardly understand that a professor should publish in the *Philological Quarterly* or *The Utah Academy Proceedings,* but the point is that Tommy Turner is quite realistic as a comic mask. At the beginning of the play he seems to be an old man: he forgets his wife's birthday, he cannot remember what kind of liquor to buy for a party, and he does not care about football games. He has accepted a stodgy kind of world sometimes thought to be characteristic of the *Atlantic Monthly.* When he learns of a message from his chairman, he anticipates a promotion, a raise in salary, and further deadening years. In the middle of the play, in the drinking scene with the young editor who precipitates the crisis of the play, Turner undergoes a ritual death. He awakens after the drinking scene with a hangover but with new energy and resolve. His wife deliberately chooses the new Tommy Turner; she says to the ex-football player, "I'm kind of scared of him. He used to be just— nice, but now he's wonderful!" When the play ends, Turner is dancing with his wife, something he has not done for ten years. He is alive again.

The narrator or the essay voice of *Let Your Mind Alone* is the *eiron*, the essays' equivalent of Tommy Turner. He does not experience ritual rebirth, but at the end of each contest he perceives an aspect of experience that is wider and more fruitful than any insight conveyed by psychologists. He does not receive a bride as a prize, but he is clearly eligible for any prize the reader wishes to grant him as victor.

Opposing the *eiron*, the impostor enters the play with a wrong idea, a crazy notion, an expanded view of himself. His entrance precipitates the comic action since the hero must meet his challenge and defeat him. Heavy fathers, bragging soldiers, or learned pedants are typical impostors in comedy. Joe Ferguson, the football player, is the impostor in *The Male Animal.* He is in *fact* an impostor since he does not explain (even to himself possibly) that he has come back because his wife is divorcing him and he wants to renew his old pursuit of Ellen Turner. The impostor is also a braggart, or he is a soldier returning from wars. Joe Ferguson is impressed with his own performance in the battle of life and his role as an ex-football hero. Ferguson attracts bands, Tommy Turner complains, as is fitting for a returned warrior. He is also willing to propose the "right" point of view that Tommy should take about the Vanzetti letter, and thus he qualifies as a self-made pedant. At the end of the play he is unmasked as a peace-loving suburbanite with a business and a mother. Again, seeing it from a distance, we discover in the play the ancient pattern of comedy.

When we turn to the essays to find the impostor figure in them, we get a surprise. He is there, but he appears in an astonishing new costume. In the impostor role Thurber invents a new comic type. He may not invent it himself, but he develops it by the examples in *Let Your Mind Alone*. My examples of the type—fathers, soldiers, pedants—are all men; Thurbers are women! Consider the female pedant, Dorothea Brande, author of *Wake Up and Live*, a woman who has "reputedly change[d] the lives of almost as many people as the Oxford Group." Another female impostor is Sadie Myers Shellow, Ph.D., who was "formerly psychologist with the Milwaukee Electric Railway & Light Company." Not only is Dr. Shellow full of foolish suggestions, but she is utterly defeated by the English language. Both of these women are caught in a lie which the voice speaking the essays exposes. With both women, Thurber opens up a whole new world of comic possibilities. Further, Thurber has not invented these women; they are absolutely real.

The comic writer in the past used women only for atmosphere or as the prize to be awarded to the hero. The wife in *The Male Animal* follows the convention. She says funny things, but her major value is to be the object of attention for Turner and Ferguson. In a society where women increasingly act, the comic writer introduces the female liar, the woman locked in her special interest. Her fixed concentration transforms her from an ordinary human into a comic liar who blocks the comic hero's full, liberal view of life. The female impostor is also possible to the American writer because of the behavior of American women. Impostors are frequently father surrogates (the Old King is father of the New King). The vitality of the American woman suggests that she will easily assume a commanding position to oppress, repress, and suppress with foolhardy aplomb. She can be defeated without engendering too much sympathy in the audience. The only predecessors Northrop Frye cites are Katharine in *The Taming of the Shrew* and some women in Molière's *Les Femmes Savantes*. Another example, at least for the first canto of the work, might be the modern mother, Donna Inez, in Byron's *Don Juan*. The type is rare everywhere but in Thurber. I believe that one of the qualities that makes "The Secret Life of Walter Mitty" such a pertinacious and enduring creation is the fact that Mrs. Walter Mitty is an example of an impostor; Mrs. Ulgine Barrows in "The Catbird Seat" is also. The lady mind experts in the first ten sketches of *Let Your Mind Alone* are superior comic creations compared to Joe Ferguson, and they are a new and surprising variation on an old design.

In the second part of *Let Your Mind Alone,* a sketch entitled "Women Go On Forever," Thurber defines the qualities that make the type possible. The familiar essay voice, with his wide view and understanding, is speaking:

> Each expert, in his fashion, has analyzed the decline of Mankind and most of them have prescribed remedies for the patient. But none of them, I believe, has detected the fact that although Man, as he is now traveling, is headed for extinction, Woman is not going with him. It is, I think, high time to abandon the loose generic term "Man," for it is no longer logically inclusive or scientifically exact. There is Man and there is Woman, and Woman is going her own way.

The fact that woman is going her own way makes her an impostor; one can almost see her fixed grin and her eye riveted to a point on the horizon. At the end of the sketch, the speaker quotes a Harvard lecturer who observes that "when women reach a certain age they seem to become immortal." Thurber concludes, "I think that he and I have got hold of something. Just what good it will do us, being males, I do not know." The good for comedy is obvious. Woman is no longer a prize awarded, an animated trophy who bears children. She is a liar, a threat, and a strong opponent to the comic hero. When he has triumphed over her, he has indeed accomplished something. If the comic mask represents a kind of immortality, she has indeed gained immortality.

Thurber's female impostors prevail in other places than those infested by woolly-minded psychologists, for the new type also appears in the second half of *Let Your Mind Alone* where Thurber reverts to his more conventional comic sketch. She is caught in some nutty idea — such as inviting grooms to bridal showers — which prevents the comic heroes from living the life that their instinct tells them they should live. Marcia Winship in "The Breaking Up of the Winships" is caught in a fixed conviction about Greta Garbo's supremacy as an actress; her husband insists that Donald Duck is superior. "The Case Against Women" begins with an impostor in full rig:

> A bright-eyed woman, whose sparkle was rather more of eagerness than of intelligence, approached me at a party one afternoon and said, "Why do you hate women, Mr. Thurberg?" I quickly adjusted my fixed grin and denied that I hated women.

Thurber's female impostors frequently get names and other little conveniences of civilization absolutely wrong, nor will they be corrected. Even Helen Hayes is forced into the role in "No Standing Room Only." Miss Hayes had the charming idea of admitting only fifty-two standees for a performance of *Victoria Regina* to celebrate the end of the first year's run of the play. It seems worth noting that Thurber's female impostors are frequently bent on changing some social convention which the male finds useful and comfortable. These females must be driven away so that the comic voice of the essay can achieve his victory and his comic celebration.

To say that Thurber invents a new comic type, the female threat to the comic hero, is extreme since other twentieth-century writers use the type. Both Peter De Vries and John Updike have examples, but the type is rare in British writing. Shaw uses female heroines, but his heroes are rarely blocked by female impostors. We think of the Battle of the Sexes as an old, old phenomenon; it probably is, but only in our times has this Battle genuinely become an integral part of comedy. The standard comedy still presents two men—such as Turner and Ferguson—engaged in a struggle which ends in the victory of one man closely identified with a hoped-for life energy; his prize is a nubile, young female. The New Woman, to use a phrase from Shaw who did not quite see the possibilities, has power, and she is also capable of self-deception and self-importance. She is able, therefore, to be a liar. I find it curious and illustrative of my point that when that very conservative institution, Hollywood, adapted "The Secret Life of Walter Mitty," Mrs. Mitty's role was completely rewritten. She became his mother! She contributes to the comedy but she does not participate in it as she does in Thurber's story. The screenwriters created a new character, young and pretty, to be the love interest and Mitty's final prize. Hollywood, and Hollywood's audience, were not ready to accept Thurber's woman as impostor.

On the other hand, the female *eiron* or comic hero is not at all unusual in Thurber or in other writers. The mother in *My Life and Hard Times* has the typical life and vitality of the comic hero and the brains to penetrate the disguises and lies of the comic opposition. Mrs. Monroe occasionally plays the role; like a comic hero-rascal she puts on an act, for example, to extricate herself and Mr. Monroe from a boring social occasion. In Thurber's late pieces, the female comic victor is all over the place; his own mother and Margery Albright in *The Thurber Album* are both females who see better and who understand life better than the men around them.

The *eiron* and the impostor are the main comic figures, but below them in importance are two other comic stereotypes or masks: the buffoon and the plain-dealer or rustic, who contribute to the general mood of good humor, the comic tone. They may even repeat the errors of the main characters in a more ridiculous form; they comment on the action, direct our response toward it, and sometimes tip and balance at the right moment so that the hero can win his advantage over the impostor.

In *The Male Animal*, Blanche Damon, wife of the English department chairman, and Myrtle Keller, wife of the representative university trustee, are buffoons setting the mood of hilarity in the first act. They contribute nothing to the action, but they carry on a funny conversation about terrible ailments. Such medical discussions are traditional in comedy. In some folk versions of the seasonal rites that comedy is based on, a learned doctor who is a comic buffoon brings the New King back to life. The eating and drinking scene (standard American cocktail party) is also traditional; the libation honors the god of comedy and encourages the rebirth of the comic hero. Blanche gets a little tipsy, and Myrtle remarks about some unknown person: "They took a stone out of her as big as a walnut." One of Blanche's lines, straight out of the blue, is "They took a pint of pus out of her." Because Blanche and her husband represent the college point of view before it is proved alive by Turner's final action, Blanche defines the dead and possibly irrelevant faculty world. She illustrates Thurber's later joke about how *some* American women (not his female impostors) are like American colleges: they both have half-dead faculties. Myrtle is thoroughly addle-pated, but unlike her husband, essentially harmless. The two women disappear after the first act; their function is to provide the hilarity, frivolity, and gaiety that is necessary and to exaggerate and emphasize the impotence of their side to the comic struggle.

Ed Keller, Myrtle's husband, also plays the role of buffoon, but he has slightly more to do in the play and stays in it until the final curtain. He is described as being "big, loud, slightly bald, . . .a prosperous real-estate man, . . .a trustee and. . .the biggest voice and the strongest hand on the Board." He is an older, exaggerated version of Joe Ferguson. He eats too much, thinks too little, and talks too loudly. He always judges the surface appearance and his mistakes contribute to the hilarity. At the end of the play, his misunderstanding of the marital arrangements (he is both pleased and embarrassed that Joe Ferguson may abduct the professor's wife) lightens the tone in preparation for the ending.

The rustics are played by the two young men in the play, Wally Myers and Michael Barnes. Wally Myers is the current hero of the football team and he ogles Joe Ferguson, apes his behavior, and hopes to be the same kind of man. He is an innocent country boy who has seen his first hero. Michael Barnes, editor of the student literary magazine, instigates the action by printing a report that Turner will courageously read the Vanzetti letter. His sophistication is a thin veneer over his essential innocence. His failure to seduce Hot Garters Gardner (or Hot-Cha-Cha Gardner in one published version of the play) and his difficulties in wooing Turner's young sister-in-law amuse us because, like Wally, he is so untried, so much the rustic on his first disaster. Wally and Michael, then, repeat the roles of Ferguson and Turner, but since the young men are so patently absurd, the audience has an additional perspective on the main contest.

The rustic also has a related form, the plain-dealer or "refuser of festivity," who defines the comedy by taking up a position at a distance from the action. This character is an outspoken advocate of a kind of moral norm, and he has the sympathy of the audience. Dr. Damon, Chairman of the English Department, is the plain-dealer in *The Male Animal.* Early in the play he resignedly expounds a doctrine of expediency that the trustees try to force on Turner. What does it matter, the chairman of the English department asks, if you do or do not read a letter? At this point in the play the tone is detached enough so that the speech confuses the audience as much as it makes sense. Later in the play, Damon unmistakably cuts through the issues to state the social norm of the new society that Turner creates at the end, the liberated and independent society of humanistic intelligence. Damon is experienced, dry, and somewhat removed; he is the man that Turner may become if he does not learn to act. He has been through the whole charade before, and his detachment contributes to the comedy in the same way as the innocence of the two boys.

The buffoons and rustics appear also in the sketches, but there they have less function since, in its economy, the sketch concentrates on the contest between the ironic narrator and the impostor who threatens him. In the vignettes illustrating and explaining the comic conclusions, the buffoons and rustics make some contribution. B. J. Winfall and Russell Soames in "How to Adjust to Your Work" are different forms of the same comic roles played by Blanche Damon and Dr. Damon. B. J. takes his employee, Soames, to Chicago on a business deal. Like Blanche Damon, B. J. is more interested in liquor than business and after three days of drinking announces that before he goes back to New York,

> I want to see a dive, a hideout, a joint. I want to see them in
> action, by God, if they ever get into action. I think most of it is
> newspaper talk. Your average gangster is a yellow cur.

B. J. gets himself into a ridiculous disguise and the two find a hide-out. B. J. behaves disgracefully. He taunts the gangsters with: "I'm two-gun Winfall from New York City!" and shouts "Anybody want anything?" It is only through Russell Soames' most "cringing, obsequious explanations and apologies" that he and B. J. manage to extricate themselves. Soames insists that they are "just drunken bums with broken hearts." The adventure illustrates the point of the essay—the "bright, hard rules of general conduct" recommended by success writers would destroy a man who follows them as B. J. Winfall does—but the adventure creates the spirit of festivity. B. J. heightens it by bumptiously joining in the action; Soames heightens it by refusing to be involved until the last desperate moment.

These minor characters—buffoons and plain dealers—appear in Thurber's sketches when the story-teller becomes strong. At the same time that they heighten the hilarity, they also echo the comic contest. In the best pieces, as in the story of B. J. Winfall or the practical jokes that Burt Scursey plays on Harry Conners, the buffoons further qualify and intensify the comic action.

The Victory at the End

Comic endings range from one extreme in which the comic victory is full and triumphant to an opposite in which the victory is so slight that it may be barely noticeable. The most ironic or bitter comedy is that in which the hero is nearly smothered by his opposition; in the romantic comedy, the victory is so complete that the hero seems to be founding a newly born society with the new life and value that he represents. Comedy ranges from one extreme in which the comic hero's very presence is a kind of lament against society for not allowing this man to live more triumphantly to the other extreme where it is almost a religious vision (recall the *Divine Comedy*), in which the comic hero redeems the society. The victory may range from a token victory, the mere fact of survival, to the victory that changes and completely reanimates the world in which it takes place. Thurber comes closest to the triumphant comedy in *The Male Animal* and, much later, in his five fairy tales.

Thurber prefers the bitter. Granting his impostors, I suspect that only small victories are possible. Is there any comic victor in *My Life and Hard Times?* The mother seems to qualify sometimes; the narrator rarely qualifies since he is nearly inundated in most contests he engages in; Grandfather's saving common sense sometimes qualifies him to near triumphs. *Let Your Mind Alone* has endings ranging from the very bitter to a point that is still considerably less than the limited victory of *The Male Animal.*

Because they are more typical of his early style, I will consider his bitter endings first. The first sketch in Part II of *Let Your Mind Alone* tells the story of "The Breaking Up of the Winships." The story begins innocently enough when the wife expresses her admiration of Greta Garbo. Marcia Winship is one of Thurber's female impostors. Like the typical impostor, her admiration for Garbo becomes an "enchantment [which] borders almost on fanaticism and sometimes even touches the edges of frenzy." The husband accepts her bondage, but finally must take arms against it. Detachment, he says, "is a necessary thread in the fabric of a woman's charm," and the loss of Marcia's detachment turns her into a comic character, an impostor. The husband cannot meet the challenge, for he, equally, loses his detachment: he insists that Donald Duck is a greater actor than Garbo! They both lie; they realize their error, but they are locked in their illogic. They settle their quarrel momentarily, but in an effort to release the tensions of the quarrel, the husband tells the story to a lady novelist. The wife, overhearing her husband's version of the story, concludes that he has gone in search of allies and thus renews her attack. The marriage falls to pieces.

Can this be called comedy? Like the "Mr. and Mrs. Monroe" sketches, it is so harsh that it denies comedy. No new society gets born at the end. The humorous society that might get born in the possibilities of Donald Duck's acting ability is destroyed with the marriage. The characters are smothered by their lie. The story looks more exactly like a tragedy with two people pursuing to the bitter end a sudden flaw in their characters, the loss of humanistic detachment or disinterest.

But the story is framed by a narrator who tells us that he "was inclined to laugh it off." Thus the Winships are separated from us by his intervening personality. At the end of the story, the Winships appear, at a further distance, in the narrator's dream. In it Gordon, Marcia and the narrator are out hunting when Marcia shoots a rabbit. On reaching the dead rabbit, they find "that it was a white rabbit and it was wearing a vest and carrying a watch." The narrator refuses to analyze the dream and tries "to forget the whole miserable business." The narrator is, again, the *eiron* or comic hero of the piece, for he sees the vestiges of a comic pattern. The male principle of victory is his perception of the *Alice in Wonderland* parallel. The Winships are involved in a tragedy, but because we see their story from the vantage point of the observer, the story has that twinge of hope and the touch of laughter in a dreadful universe that makes it all bearable.

At a deeper level of bitterness is "After the Steppe Cat, What?" It is a typical example of the many sketches that Thurber wrote on a twentieth-century drive to destroy ourselves and our environment. Few older writers ever tried to get comedy out of such cosmic and dreadful topics. In this essay a wasteland appears in the depredation of the earth that the technician seems bent upon. The specific example is a newspaper report that animals common to the steppes have appeared, as a result of reclamation projects, in eastern Germany. If man's behavior destroys even the lowly steppe cat, then what hope is there? The victory is not even human; it is simply an animal persistence.

In "An Outline for Scientists" a pseudo-scientist (one step above the technician) is the impostor. The narrator—Thurber himself, bedridden because of a bee sting—reads a scientific encyclopedia. He is confounded by the "simple" explanation of Einstein's theories, but he is astounded by the inaccuracy of a comment on bloodhounds. He concludes with Thurber's Law, "which is that scientists don't really know anything about anything." Again, the victory is weak; one does not end scientific over-simplification by a humanistic quip:

> I have never liked or trusted scientists very much, and I think now that I know why: they are afraid of bloodhounds. They must, therefore, be afraid of frogs, jack rabbits, and the larger pussycats. . .
>
> Bloodhounds are sometimes put on the trail of old lost ladies or little children who have wandered away from home. When a bloodhound finds an old lady or a little child, he instantly swallows the old lady or the little child whole, clothes and all. This is probably what happened to Charlie Ross, Judge Crater, Agnes Tufverson, and a man named Colonel Appel, who disappeared at the battle of Shiloh. . . .
>
> I guess that's all I have to say to the scientists right now, except boo!

Because scientists do sometimes fail to understand a bloodhound, the reader's heart lifts up. This machine of infallibility, this scientific realm of Pooh-bahs, cannot see the plain facts. Scientists too lie. They too can be routed by a male animal just as trustees and foolish lady psychologists. We can say *Boo!* It is not much but it is an action.

In two other pieces, however, the male animal acts with greater strength. Their endings lie about equidistant in the continuum between pure complaint and that longed-for vision of a new and better world that we seem to see at the end of the play. The first is "Doc Marlow," a sketch of a Thurber Falstaff who outrageously cheats his way through life, dispensing an elixir known as Blackhawk Liniment. He sells his liniment at thirty-five cents a bottle, but the narrator is assured by trustworthy evidence that Doc cannot make much profit. Furthermore, he generously gives away many bottles. He does make a little extra money cheating at cards. He even cheats his kind-hearted landlady who allows him to gets months behind in his rent. He cheats a pleasant middle-aged couple out of one hundred dollars they pay him for a worthless Cadillac. Two days before his death, he confesses that he even cheated the narrator by using a coin with "heads on both sides" when they tossed to pay for a soda on a warm day. At the very moment of his death, Doc Marlowe is still playing his brainy, opportunistic tricks.

In "The Wood Duck" Thurber's comedy comes about as close toward a new vision as the essays in *Let Your Mind Alone* can come, and again the vision comes to us through an animal, this time a wild duck that has made a home for itself at a farmstead. Stopping at a farm to buy cider, a man and his wife see the wild wood duck. They admire the wild creature and feel a yearning identification with it, but while they watch, the duck strays too close to the noisy, oily, concrete highway, and is swept into the traffic. At first the onlookers fear that the bird is dead, but it comes to its feet "like a person who has been abruptly wakened and doesn't know where he is." When an old setter dog attacks it, the duck makes a desperate effort to escape to the woods. The onlookers restrain the dog, and the duck disappears. Later in the evening the man and wife return to ask if the bird has come back. The husband goes to ask and then comes back to the car.

> "Well," I said, "He's back." "I'm glad he is, in a way," said my
> wife. "I hated to think of him all alone out there in the woods."

The mindless force of the modern world, represented by the highway with its onrushing traffic, cannot drive away what the husband calls "a marvel." The duck confers a grace on their life by the simple act of its life. When the duck leaves the farm, some grace is lost; when he returns, he brings meaning. At least one thing has not been destroyed. Thus the presence of the bird signals to us the distant melody of the *Comos*, the hymn of life.

Typically in comic action the dramatist brings his action as close to catastrophe as he can, and then reverses it quickly. In *The Male Animal* the audience is convinced that Tommy Turner will accede to the trustee's demand and that he will lose his wife to Jumping-Joe. In "The Wood Duck" the man and wife leave, fearing that the bird will never return. Near the end of "After the Steppe Cat, What?" civilization itself is sterile and dead. At the close of "Doc Marlowe" we witness not only a death but the seeming death of a young boy's confidence in his fellow man. The comic writer brings his audience as close to failure, as close to tragedy, as he can, and then swiftly a vital principle of action appears and enables us to feel the resurrection of life energy. The ending of tragedy is inevitable; granting the facts, no other end is possible. Comedy has no inevitable conclusion except for rebirth and rejuvenation. In Thurber, the new birth takes place inside the mind of the reader when he shares the narrator-hero's vision.

Thurber's comedies nevertheless reach their ending with appropriate naturalness. Nothing is arranged. A lesser comedy would permit the Winships to escape from their respective bondage to Garbo and Donald Duck. Thurber, however, never asks us to do violence to our common sense. The wood duck might well have been only injured; Doc Marlowe would play his tricks up to the end. The freedom of the essay or sketch allows Thurber more room to bring his reader into the perception. Moreover Thurber never exaggerates his impostors to achieve his comedy. They are always funny, but they are funny because of their own nature. Thurber gives us ,no sense that he distorts them to make them grotesque. It seems to me that his comedy is the art of the possible.

I have used the model of ancient comedy to see how Thurber varied and changed a given archetype. While Thurber's basic struggle is the same as that in Greek comedy, his contestants wear different clothes and his endings celebrate a life in the mind. I have used the model, then, as a heuristic device. Thurber can stand without it, but with it *we* can see how the artist has played a new song. We still celebrate witty man's struggle with his universe, but we require a new victory. We do not arrange ceremonies to insure that crops will grow, rivers flow, and women bear children; we fertilize our crops, dam our rivers, and seek out gynecologists to study our reproductive organs. Our danger, a more terrifying danger, lies not so much in imponderable forces of weather or reproduction, but in those imponderable forces of our own nature that restrain us from the life that our soul needs. In Thurber the struggle has moved from the universe of natural forces into the universe of the mind.

Thurber's *The Last Flower: A Parable in Pictures* (1939) shows once more the old struggle between the forces of death and destruction and the new force of life that comedy must celebrate. The text is too brief for summary but the text and drawings recreate the battle of life found in comedy from the seasonal rites to the music hall routines. At the end of Thurber's parable, the Thirteenth World War has destroyed everything but one man, one woman, and one flower. Thurber's ending is both bitter and triumphant. Life still perserveres, but we also sense the imponderable nature of man that traps him in aggressive, destructive habits. In ordinary sublunary experience we sense little possibility of redemption or rebirth, and yet the fact of the flower is a triumph. I recently saw a production of the revue, *A Thurber Carnival*, in which a middle-aged woman standing before an easel recited the words in a flat, neutral, sad, but strangely alive, voice. She was dressed in grey, and she wore flat heels. Her face, as she turned to the audience and then back to the easel, was almost expressionless. When she finished the words, saying that all was destroyed "except one man, one woman, and one flower," she turned the easel to show the Thurber flower. The audience gasped. The stem is so fragile that it can barely support the flower. I have no idea what kind of flower it is. Everything has been removed but the simple fact of life itself. Only life survives, but life is the subject of comedy from Aristophanes to Thurber.

V

✺

The Beast
in the Marges of the Mind

A weekly discussion group decided to purchase a tape recorder
to have a more permanent record of its deliberations. No one in
the group had ever heard his own voice and each was very uncertain about his ability to say anything meaningful about the subjects under discussion. The recording of their discussion sounded
like a giggle factory. No one said anything very witty, but every
attempt at wit produced gales of laughter. The group was so nervous
about the machine and so uncertain of its own sophistication
that laughter was the only defense. Everyone knows of a fat man
who laughs at his size or a cripple who laughs at his own affliction
to fend off possible embarrassment. A group of people stuck in
an elevator that has been caught between floors may break into
unreasonable laughter. In all these cases the laughter is a defense
against one's sense of insecurity. It follows, therefore, that uncertainties and confusions are very potent materials for the comic
artist. If he can recreate the sense of inadequacy induced by the
threat of having one's voice recorded on the tape, the sense of fat-
ness, affliction, or danger that precipitates laughter, then laughter
may be triggered by a small expenditure of wit. Sexual topics
stimulate laughter not only because sex is funny but because the
subject arouses so many fears, frustrations and inhibitions. The
comic writer, therefore, will seek out subjects which embrace fears,
frustrations, and uncertainties.

Francis Hackett's "Odd Man Out" (in *On Judging Books*,

pp. 29-40) agrees with the notion that comedy derives from social tension, but Hackett ends by resorting to biography rather than art when he claims that Thurber uses "humor in a peculiar defensive role" to hide his own idealistic sensitivity. Thurber laughs, according to Hackett, to cover the wound made when society threatens to ridicule Thurberean feeling. Thus, to understand Thurber's comedy we need to know the particular aspects of his personality that make him vulnerable to this potential ridicule. The argument is persuasive, since Thurber does create sensitive men like George Bidwell, Charlie Deshler, Mr. Pendly and Mr. Bruhl and invites us to laugh when these men are under attack.* Thurber's friends report that anger and rage were basic to his character, and Mark Van Doren attests to that rage in his poem for Thurber, "Anger Is, Anger Was." To argue, however, that Thurber's comedy is merely the result of his Ohio sensitivity is to demean both Thurber and his comedy. The Sad Clown Theory of comedy reduces comedy to a social accident, a product of erring society's persecution of the poor clown. It is a theory which, as we shall see, falls short of accounting for the purpose and achievement of the comic *artist.*

Granted that individuals use comedy and laughter as a means of defense and release in situations of fear, embarrassment or danger, the comic artist goes way beyond this. Instead of merely responding to these situations by laughter, he manipulates them and uses them as the source of a genuine art. We should care less about Thurber's own sensitivities than about his ability to make laughter possible for us by deliberately choosing subjects that will create nervous, unsettling and unbearable tensions. This is not to deny that Thurber's own sensitivity is great and is a very powerful ingredient in his comedy. But there are sensitive Ohioans all over the place and they are by no means all comic artists. To define the sensitivity that Thurber deliberately creates will provide a powerful means for exploring the aims and purposes of his comedy. And, as I have been claiming all along, defining this tension that Thurber uses for his comedy also enables us to see how his comedy changes and develops. He starts in the 1930's with sensitive and

---

*And Thurber supports the idea in an essay on George Kaufman: "The writer of humor and comedy is by nature a complicated human being, and the craft he practices is in part a necessary counterbalance to God knows how many different kinds of inner conflict." ("The Man Who Was Comedy" in *Credos and Curios*).

inept men who create their own predicaments because of their sensitivity; we are ready to laugh because we too are sensitive and know that our sensitivity would get us into trouble if we allowed it to. As he develops he turns more and more to look at the mind that creates the sensitivity.

Thurber's comedy, especially that of the 1940's, consummately exploits fears, uncertainties, and inhibitions about the relationships between the mind and the world. Stated so baldly his subject looks unpromising, but the mock-epigraph for *The Beast in Me*, an epigraph supposedly written by Douglas Bryce, one of the characters in one of the stories, makes comedy out of the mind's ability, or inability, to link fact and thought:

> ...but I am concerned with the beast inside, the beast that haunts the moonlit marges of the mind, never clearly seen, never wholly lost to view, never leaving, in its wanderings, pawprints sharp enough to follow, or strange and promising enough, it well may be, to lure the wary hunter from the surer spoor of bigger game.

Is the beast, or are we, any place in particular? Thurber's comedy, like the beast, haunts the "moonlit marges of the mind." It issues from our inability to distinguish truth from falsehood by any other means than by that uncertain agent, the mind itself. Notice that Thurber's sentence itself shifts before our eyes. Although it appears to be prose, it contains a rhythm very close to verse. I want to print the words this way:

> But I am concerned with the beast inside,
> The beast that haunts
> The moonlit marges of the mind,
> Never clearly seen,
> Never wholly lost to view,
> Never leaving, in its wanderings,
> Pawprints sharp enough to follow, or,
> Strange and promising enough, it well may be,
> To lure the wary hunter
> From the surer spoor of bigger game.

In the moonlit marges of the mind, the psychologist or the poet plays his wonderful, frightening, and exciting game. It is the game of civilization that Thurber plays when he writes the epigraph and all the stories in the book.

The Last Flower, a fable with drawings about the twelfth and thirteenth world wars, inaugurates the "high middle period" of Thurber's writing. The period deserves the name *high* because of his increased sense of the mind as a threat and because of his increased ability to dramatize that threat. *My World and Welcome to It* (1942), the six new stories in *The Thurber Carnival* (1945), and *The Beast in Me and Other Animals* (1948) include the essays, stories and sketches of this high period.* Although Thurber was losing his eyesight, the time between 1939 and 1950 was a period of intense creativity. "The imagination," Thurber commented to an interviewer, "doesn't go blind." The imagination, I want to add, can see the beast inside.

The tension or the drama comes from three sources. First it comes from within the mind of the individual who deludes himself. This placement is familiar in Thurber. In "The Black Magic of Barney Haller" and "The Remarkable Case of Mr. Bruhl" (both in *The Middle-Aged Man*), fears and ideas with their own nature drive the characters to distraction (and death). The idea is brilliantly exploited in *My World and Welcome to It.* A second category of threat comes from the public mind, the intellectual clichés and political habits never wholly lost to view and never clearly seen but surely keeping us from the spoor of bigger game. A third category is the threat from our efforts to discover meaning in our familiar truths, the little ways and habits of our own behavior. In this last category, Thurber gets very close to enunciating a code for the artist that his own work justifies.

The Beast in the Individual

Tommy Turner triumphs because he has wit and luck; in the sketches Thurber wrote in the 1930's, the greater wit and intelligence of the narrator (or the essayist's voice) penetrates the fog of psychologists, grammarians, and sexologists. Comedy, from the most ancient records to the most ephemeral contemporary joke, shows a witty rascal able to put fools of any stripe in place. In addition to varying his endings, Thurber also varies the forces

---

Fables for Our Time (1939) and *Further Fables of Our Time* (1956) belong, chronologically and thematically, to this period as do the five fairy tales, *Many Moons* (1943), *The Great Quillow* (1944), *The White Deer* (1945), *The Thirteen Clocks* (1950), and *The Wonderful O* (1957). Subsequent chapters discuss these works.

(the fools) that attack his heroes. If in the old comedy the threat comes from outside forces, in our world the threat comes from minds that create destructive machines, suburban comfort, government directives, or directives on how radio drama should be written. We laugh not because we need release from sexual uncertainty, religious pressure, or cosmic forces beyond our ken, but to find release from tension created by the mind. The word *mind* is amorphous, but I mean by it the ability to construct patterns of meaning (or non-meaning) which enslave. A view of the world, such as Mrs. Mitty's, may be perfectly logical and right but it may also stultify. "I am concerned with the beast inside," Thurber writes, and his words refer to the drawings of beasts included in the book rather than the beast of the mind that I am insisting on. He says that the beasts "emerged from the shameless breeding ground of the idle mind and they are obviously not going anywhere in particular." The beasts, however, could not be omitted. He includes, for example, "A female Shriek rising out of the Verbiage to attack a female Swoon." They serve "as the legendary thread that stubbornly unravels the whole." In addition to these drawings, the book includes beasts in the idle minds of his fools. In the stories, the beasts are the comfort in American society and the freedom of a permissive society to invent stupidities. The beasts are the arbitrary and intransigent forces ranging from the comforts of Mrs. Mitty through the conventions of Hollywood, to the clichés of mass culture.

Consider "The Secret Life of Walter Mitty," the best known of Thurber's fictions, in *My World and Welcome to It.* The comedy exists in the tension created by the wife's world-view, her beast, as opposed to Mitty's view. The wife is the threat against Mitty's free and desirable heroism. The wife, we know, is sensible in her judgment. Mitty should drive more slowly on the weekly shopping trip to Waterbury. He should remember his overshoes. He should sit where Mrs. Mitty can find him when she is finished shopping. Civilization requires such order, and Thurber's characters, even as they mutter "Things close in," nevertheless must accept the order and pattern of the highly complicated constructions which make civilization. The story would not be funny if Mitty and his reader did not recognize the equity of Mrs. Mitty's directions. Mitty is caught between his wife's effort to reduce life to a dull

platitude and his own desire for larger freedom. Mitty cannot
violate his wife's order because he has made it. He has not, of
course, in fact made it, but he acquiesces to it. It is reasonable
and comfortable.

We want freedom and yet we have to accept order, hoping for
"surer spoor of bigger game." We want to be Walter Mitty, venturing in the imagination, and yet we have to be Mrs. Mitty shopping:
on the one hand, noble folly in Mitty but, on the other, base wisdom in Mrs. Mitty. The choice in comedy is often between body
(Mrs. Mitty and her base wisdom) and soul, but Thurber's choice
is so much more complicated. Since the body is omnipresent and
powerful, Mitty feels his victory only in his imagined adventures
as a Navy pilot, a surgeon, a lawyer, and finally as true patriot
dying before a firing squad. He obtains his freedom because his
mind can invent a larger world than his wife's mind can.

Or to put it another way, Mitty is a satisfying and universal
modern comic figure because he is the comfortable suburban man,
living in his split-level house with all the convenience of bar, bed,
and storage bin. He wants not. A human and noble urge tells him
to yearn for heroic action, but a "beast" prevents him from obtaining his freedom. He yearns for noble folly as he accepts the
base wisdom of his wife's comfort. Often in comedy an arbitrary
law is destroyed by comic action. In older comedy, the law is frequently absurd, but in Thurber, while still arbitrary, it is reasonable
and in accord with experience. The arbitrary law of the wife's
order and comfort has not the slightest inkling of noble folly. The
story would collapse had Mrs. Mitty ordered her husband to slow
down to save tires for the war effort. Arbitrarily she adheres to
her reasonable aim of comfort and Mitty defeats it. The fact that
the character triumphs over a law of comfort without a chip of
complaint or a Christ symbol of ancient hopes is a measure of
Thurber's success as an artist. He convinces us with the attitudes
and symbols available from his society.

Thurber amuses his reader because he frees the reader from
pressures of the mind, but in "The Secret Life of Walter Mitty,"
he allows us to indulge in a displaced victory of mind over body.
Mitty triumphs over a dead, sterile, old form of life that we want
to disavow. We take pleasure in seeing Mrs. Mitty so thoroughly
hoodwinked by Mitty's mad and wonderful inventions. The inven-

tions are wrong and implausible (a doctor reports a victim dying of coreopsis, the name of a common garden flower), but they have a wonderful authenticity like the fantastic inventions of physicists, chemists, or engineers. The scientists and the engineers frighten or confuse us; how pleasant then to see their characteristic behavior as a subject of laughter. Envying their power to invent, we find pleasure in identifying with Mitty as he too invents and structures his world of noble folly. The story gives flesh to our tensions — our fears, hopes, expectations — and provides a way to act them out (as much as reading a story allows us to act out) in a kingdom of the imagination where the immediate consequences do not matter. Brains invent bombs; stories enable us to experience without suffering the hazard of arbitrary beasts of our own mind.

The sketches in *My World and Welcome to It* frequently use for their arbitrary law fools who push the freedom of an easy, permissive society to an absurd conclusion. An American lady in "The Macbeth Murder Mystery" reads *Macbeth,* against all fact, as if it were a murder story. In "The Preoccupation of Mr. Peffifoos," a telephone official gratuitously changes telephone numbers. In "Backward and Downward with Mr. Punch," the cheap and superior nineteenth-century freedom of *Punch* runs rampant over facts. "The Man Who Hated Moonbaum" tells the story of a Hollywood director anxious to traduce Tristram and Isolde. The freedom to think and act in error leads these characters astray until the noble folly of the comic hero in each story asserts itself in comic victory.

One of the stories in *My World and Welcome to It,* "The Whip-Poor-Will" illustrates the capacity of comedy to give release from uncertainty about the mind's ability to derive meaning from experience. At the surface the story seems hardly comic at all since it ends with the central character committing a triple murder and then suicide. Thurber comments in an interview that the story has "an element of anger. . .a grim fear" in it. The grim fear is precisely the arbitrary rule of mind from which the hero must free himself. Unlike Mitty, who can free himself by counter-invention of noble folly, this hero strikes out against his enemy and murders it. The comic hero is Mr. Kinstrey, a man awakened very early each morning by the sound of a whip-poor-will's call very close to his summer home. He recalls hearing the bird's call at home in Ohio, but he had never heard it so near nor so persistently. He tells his wife, but she offers him little sympathy. He tells his servants, but they remember that the bird's call portends death. His wife patronizingly reports that a small child has adjusted to the bird's cry, but a postal officer reports that a woman once tried to burn the island to get rid of the birds. No one can be persuaded to pay serious attention to the man's agony until, in desperation, Kinstrey slays his two servants, his wife, and himself. A police officer investigating the deaths hears the bird and recalls the superstition. A second officer, dull like the wife, says, "Take more'n a whippoor-will to cause a mess like that." The story is, nevertheless, comic.

The arbitrary law is represented by the wife who, like Mrs. Mitty, prefers the comfort and ease of her own world view. Mrs. Kinstrey pooh-poohs her husband's fears. She cuts down on his coffee and calls him a weakling. She cannot believe in her husband's suffering. Her world is comfortable, ordered and clean. On the other hand, to her husband, the bird's "sound was all around you, incredibly loud and compelling and penetrating"; it is a "brazen-breasted bird" which is "murdering sleep." The husband's color images are bright (a fire bell, bright light, bright as a flag), but the wife's color images are cool or neutral (gray, white piqué, gray hospital). He is agitated; she is comfortable. He is driven to murder, paradoxically, as the only way to assert his living perception of unease. The murders and suicide vindicate in a terrible and ironic way the truth of human sensitivity he tries to express.

As with *The Last Flower,* the laughter may be a nervous release more than genuine laughter. We feel, however, the spasm of life in Kinstrey's death. His wife is dead already in the sense that she cannot feel. The comedy ends when the impostor is destroyed, when the absurdity of the wife's law is destroyed. If Kinstrey were a real, individualized person, then the story would not be comedy. If the wife were real, then she would be a ghoul. Fortunately both of them are pasteboard masks suitable to comedy. The servants are comic servants. They are not stabbed by butcher knives; once we turn our backs, they will come back to life again just as the duelist in Thurber's "Touché" cartoon will put his head back on. In the meantime, the point has been made that the easy comfortable solution is not enough; there is a beast inside

Kinstrey and attention must be paid to it. It is a horror story and it is not humorous, but it is a story perfectly appropriate in a collection such as *My World and Welcome to It* because it makes the same point that the comedies do. "A Friend to Alexander," in the same collection, is about a man dying of a heart attack, and it too makes the point of the other comic and more humorous pieces: ideas may be powerful and real, objective threats.

One of the most complicated sketches in *My World and Welcome to It* is the brilliant opening piece, "What Do You Mean, It 'Was' Brillig?" The essay also questions the power of mind, but in a less sensational manner than "The Whip-Poor-Will." Thurber is at work when a colored maid, Della, enters his room to announce, "They are here with the reeves." Thurber attempts repeatedly to derive meaning from the woman's malapropisms. Although Della gets nearly everything wrong, her fuzziness has a mad accuracy. Della, for example, asks where Thurber is from, and when he tells her Semantics, Ohio, Della remembers that there is one also in Massachusetts. "'The one I mean,' I told her 'is bigger and more confusing.' 'I'll bet it is,' said Della."

Della's comic usurpation of language requires, on the one hand, a logic and an order to language (base wisdom), but on the other hand a freedom to invent. If a speaker were bound to the dictionary, he could not communicate new meaning since the dictionary records only old practice. If a speaker creates a language, then he runs the risk of speaking gibberish. Della sees her world freshly and uniquely, but if we all saw the world so freshly, communication would be impossible. In another sketch in *My World,* Thurber receives a message which reads, "I tried to see you in December. . .but the timekeeper said you were in Florida." ("The Gentleman in 916") The message sends Thurber off in terror; maybe a timekeeper is watching him. At the end of "What Do You Mean, It 'Was' Brillig?" Della explains to Thurber that her husband works "into a dove-wedding," a statement that conveys nothing. The mind, however, is haunted by the fear that, like the timekeeper, the phrase may hide some meaning that language has never grasped before. Like Mrs. Mitty, Della takes the easy comfortable way. Thurber's desirable society, the society striving to free itself from arbitrary law, is caught between Della's freedom and the hero's need for order! Again Thurber complicates the expected pattern. In the normal course of comedy, Della should triumph because of her freedom, but this comedy reverses the pattern and gives the victory to order. We cannot wish it another way, for Della's freedom is a crippling freedom that destroys law and sense. Thurber's victory is a freedom within law that delights and surprises.

Once comedy (and much of it still does) existed in the tension between public morality and private freedom, public law and individual desire. In Thurber's comedies the struggle moves inside the mind since a commonly agreed upon public morality and law do not exist. Because the mind creates its categories, the mind is the true area for modern comedy. The struggle is now between convenience and ease and the right of the inner life to exist in the comfortable world of suburbia. The comedies in *My World and Welcome to It* are poised between base wisdom and noble folly. Noble folly of·the mind triumphs in Mitty's dream, in Kinstrey's shocking action, and in Thurber's discovery of meaning in Della's malapropisms.

The Beast in the Cliché

From the retrospective view of *The Thurber Carnival,* a collection of his best stories up to 1945, we can easily survey the variety of intellectual impostors that threaten the comic society.

A sketch from *Let Your Mind Alone,* entitled "Sex ex Machina," combines the complications of sex, theories of the mind, automobiles, and poodles; Thurber is particularly good on the automobile or any form of gadgets that prey upon modern man:

> There goes a man who picked up one of those trick matchboxes that whir in your hands; there goes a woman who tried to change a fuse without turning off the current; and yonder toddles an ancient who cranked an old Reo with the spark advanced. Every person carries in his consciousness the old scar, or the fresh wound, of some harrowing misadvanture with a contraption of some sort. . . .I have discerned. . .a natural caution in a world made up of gadgets that whir and whine and whiz and shriek and sometimes explode.

It is no wonder that Thurber's hero is so jumpy, so often unable to move against his enemy. The impostor has the naked power of

Jack Smurch—the round-the-world pilot of "The Greatest Man in the World" (in *The Middle-Aged Man*)—that cannot be meshed with humanistic intelligence and feeling. The enemy is the comfort of platitudes that see obvious meaning (like the wife in "The Secret Life of Walter Mitty" or in "The Whip-Poor-Will") instead of significant and sensitive meaning. The impostor is the substitution of abstract thought which mangles life into a law, a statement, a piece of advice. This last impostor takes memorable form in Thurber's essays on inspirationalists who explain How to Win Approval for Everything You Want to Do by Shady Tricks Which I Can Teach You (in *Let Your Mind Alone*).

The comic writer, as is evident from the collection of stories Thurber revives in *The Thurber Carnival,* relies upon stereotypes and clichés of our everyday world. Thurber exploits types and ideas of second-rate movies. All of the impostors in the new pieces in *The Thurber Carnival* have walked off the stage of drawing room comedies, spy movies, detective stories, or folk dramas into Thurber's comic world where they are used as convenient and recognizable arbitrary law for comic exploitation. These people *are* public clichés. Thus "The Lady on 142" has impostors and a situation drawn from a bad spy movie. The hero is a nervous husband traveling twenty minutes down the line on a train. Waiting in the station he overhears a stationmaster's conversation:

> I was opening a pack of cigarettes [the familiar action of the spy movie hero] when I heard the stationmaster talking on the phone again. This time his words came out clearly. He kept repeating one sentence. He was saying, 'Conductor Reagon on 142 has the lady the office was asking about.' The person on the other end of the line did not appear to get the meaning of the sentence. The station-master repeated it and hung up. For some reason, I figured that he did not understand it either.

From this clue, the nervous husband immediately presumes that spies are loose. They are palpable—in his imagination. He imagines that his wife and he are captured and taken off to a hideout where a sophisticated leader, a manic chauffeur, and a beautiful contact agent (who had been sitting behind him on the train) persecute them.

Another story, "The Catbird Seat" also reads like a script for a movie; it begins in a tobacconist's shop on Times Square and moves through all of the familiar sets with which Hollywood has furnished our mind. "Memoirs of a Drudge" transports us to a Middle Western rural parlor. A scholar has commented that Thurber spent several years of drudgery on newspapers in Columbus, New York, and France. Thurber speaks as a crusty, rocking-chair philosopher reminiscing "When the womenfolks were washing up the supper dishes and setting them to dreen." The dialect word *dreen* crystalizes the setting. In fact, Thurber had not drudged; he led a life of high excitement, a life which contrasts oddly with the mock-persona of a cracker-barrel philosopher. In "The Cane in the Corridor" we are on the set of a drawing room comedy. The platitudinous and familiar setting establishes the arbitrary law of mind which the comic hero must extirpate himself from in order to win his comic victory.

"The Catbird Seat" dramatizes the threat to society that comes from unthinking reductionism. Reductionism is undoubtedly an ugly word, and yet it describes the action that Mrs. Ulgine Barrows (the impostor) undertakes. She is an efficiency expert. She claims to observe office practice from some special niche of insight and to be able to make it more efficient. Her foolish attempt to play the role of a brave new god initiates the comic action. Clearly she is a liar. She knows nothing about business. Erwin Martin, the hero, has worked as "head of the filing department" for twenty-two years, but now she prepares to work "a monstrous magic" on the filing department of F & S. When she came into the office, "confusion got its foot in the door."

The office of F & S is a microcosm, a universe in small. Erwin Martin, we are informed, has very little life of his own beside his work in the office. He works from eight-thirty until five-thirty, and his life away from the office is merely rest and preparation to return. He has no wife or family. After a mock trial in his mind, he sets out to murder Mrs. Barrows. "Mr. Martin could no longer doubt that the finger was on his beloved department. Her pickaxe was on the upswing, poised for the first blow." We are back at the archetypal pattern of comedy. The hero, the *eiron*, is threatened by an impostor who seeks to destroy his society. The only response is murder.

That Mrs. Barrows deserves to be murdered is clear from her behavior. We know her chiefly by her use of a baseball announcer's phrases in every context. The phrase, "to be sitting in the catbird seat," *i.e.,* to be in a position of power, had, in 1937, the freshness of an apt and vivid metaphor, but the original perception loses all its bloom in Mrs. Barrows' repetition. Mrs. Barrows is utterly insensitive to what her new regimen is doing and she is also insensitive to her repetition of public clichés. All life, we thus know, is gone from Mrs. Barrows; she attempts to reduce the living, vibrant quality of life to a few clichés. She does not think; she cannot live.

I do not want to make the comedy a moral allegory; nevertheless Mrs. Barrows is a familiar figure both in our world and in comedy. In the world, she is the expert who does not know the heart and working of human endeavor. In comedy, she is another form of Mrs. Mitty with her civilized order, efficiency, and accomplishment. She is Mrs. Kinstrey who cannot understand a husband who wakes to hear the whip-poor-will. In comedy and in experience, Mrs. Barrows is that power in the modern mind which depersonalizes and dehumanizes our world. She is so funny because she is utterly set in her direction, her clichés, her arbitrary comic law. And she is terrible enough to make any reader nervous and ready for comic release.

Erwin Martin's victory over this impossible woman is, like Walter Mitty's, a private victory. Erwin Martin is the only person (beside the reader, of course) who knows the true victory. Martin does not win anything more than release; if he were to tell how he conquered Mrs. Barrows, if he were to reveal his trick, he would lose his battle. He is Prufrock condemned to act only in the theater of his mind.

The impostor in the new stories of *The Thurber Carnival* has a recognizable reality, a basis in experience. We have all suffered from the efficient Mrs. Ulgine Barrows or the mad suspicion that the world is really a spy movie. Thurber's impostors commit their acts in public, but the victory that the hero wins is a private victory without the familiar and expected song of the *Comos.* The hero knows his victory, and his reader shares it with him, but the drama has been internalized in the moonlit marges of the mind.

The Beast in Society

The Beast in Me (1948) moves further into the affairs of man, and yet the struggle is still inside man. Mrs. Ulgine Barrows may be a representative of all the physicians, nurses, teachers, chemists, efficiency experts and knowledgeable men and women, like Miss Amy Lighter in Thurber's parody of James in "The Beast in the Dingle." In judging human experience from within their limited, comically arbitrary perception of the world, they destroy the essential quality of life. Thurber's impostors in *The Beast in Me* acquire a more overt public character. The impostors are radio clichés, gossip columnists, large central government, and pseudo-scientific generalizations that are glib but have only the vaguest shadow of approximation to the truth. His fools come from the world of mass thought like Mrs. Barrows but this mass thought has the imprimatur of commercial success. The fools stifle the noble. They want no subtlety or grace in their lives.

"The Waters of the Moon" presents as its threat an editor discussing why American writers lose their powers in middle age. The cause, he believes, "is to be found in syphilophobia, prostatitis, early baldness, peptic ulcer, edentulous cases, true and hysterical impotence, and spreading of the metatarsals." The editor asks the questions with "his laboratory glint" and "the expression of a chemist absorbed in abstruse formulae." He looks at Thurber as if the latter were "the precipitate of a moderately successful test-tube experiment." Eventually the editor leaves the party where the action takes place because "People are beginning to sing," that is, they are indulging in a kind of lyricism utterly foreign to his nature. Further, he is not able to detect Thurber's fraudulent stories about American writers who support his hypothesis. The editor believes any lie that fits his absurd theory until he penetrates the hoax and discovers "what a flaw in the verisimilitude was there!" With Thurber is "a lady chaoticist" from whom Thurber is taken to meet the famous editor and to whom Thurber returns at the end of the piece. She is the prize that the hero wins after defeating the editor. Her living chaos contrasts with the dead order of the editor. She is also practically the only woman in *The Beast in Me* who comes out unscathed.

The impostor, the editor with the *idée fixe* (the arbitrary law which must be destroyed), balances beautifully with the comic lyricism of Thurber's own invention. Thurber quickly invents three case histories to prove the editor's point. As with Walter Mitty, the stories have a springing vitality of plausibility about them. The final story is about Douglas Bryce ("I had thought the name up fast") who supposedly wrote the book quoted in the epigraph of *The Beast in Me*. Bryce's last book, according to Thurber's invention, was to have been a biography of a man in the street, entitled "Let Twenty Pass." The twenty-first man turned out to be Lawrence Stone, a slightly deaf mining engineer, who misunderstands the whole idea as "a shockingly complex plan to seize the major networks." Unfortunately the editor happens to know that the one hundred and second line of Browning's "Caliban Upon Setebos" reads "Let twenty pass and stone the twenty-first."

The innocent invention, fabricated to drive the editor out of his neat explanation, is not so innocent as it appears. If we read the story solemnly, it is the *cri-de-coeur* of the artist tied down to the trivia of the editor's sterile questing after nothing. American writers do not go sterile, for Thurber is fifty-three (according to the story) when he invents this one, but American writers may very well go sterile because of the impossible demands placed upon them. The enemy is the world which wants its little concept of fact demonstrated; Thurber prefers some finer illusion.

In other pieces in *The Beast in Me* the enemy is seen as the national sport of hunting spies and subversives. In "The Glass of Fashion," "Exhibit X," and "The Dewey Dewey Fog," Thurber comically exploits official investigations of thought. "The Glass of Fashion" is a statement to a Congressional Committee investigating Thurber for not reporting earnings made "posing" in New York restaurants. A newspaper columnist has reported that head waiters in New York arrange their famous patrons just as carefully as window dressers in department stores. The piece begins,

In the present Era of Suspicion, it is a wise citizen who disproves any dark rumors and reports of his secret thoughts and activities before they can be twisted into charges of disloyalty by the alert and skillful minds now dedicated to that high-minded and patriotic practice.

"Exhibit X" describes the relaxed security arrangements made during the first war when Americans ". . .naively feared the enemy more than they feared one another." In "The Glass of Fashion" Thurber apologizes for youthful indiscretions; he excuses himself because he "was only forty-six at the time," a statement which recalls the pleas of those who excused political misconduct on the grounds of youth.

The political statements are paralleled by fears that man is impermanent because of his propensity to believe his own lies. "My Friend Domesticus" wonders if the cricket not only presages the coming of winter but the coming end of men. In other pieces, he feels "the precarious nature of the world situation" in the "awful and magnificent light of the atomic era." In "Am Not I Your Rosalind?" characters speak into a recording device which they will leave for the "lucky people of the future, digging around in the atomic rubble." The beast is in the society like an incubus.

In *The Beast in Me* Thurber twice discusses radio's feeding of desire and insensitivity. The first piece, entitled "Thix," is a comic discussion of juvenile radio programs with a burlesque illustration in which a lisping six-year-old (thus the title) captures Major André, the Revolutionary War spy. The second is a seventy-page profile, in *New Yorker* journalistic style, of radio soap opera, its origin and present position. Both pieces remind one of Lewis Mumford's astringent disgust in *The City in History* at the games arranged for the masses in Rome. Mumford calls the games a mass playing with the genitalia. While Thurber does not speak so forthrightly, he has much the same opinion of radio.

"Soapland" is chiefly interesting for what it has to say about art in mass society. "Thix" is more witty and fun, but "Soapland" is more thorough. It is the closest thing to Thurber's artistic credo. The profile focuses directly on two threats: (1) the threat of insensitivity and (2) the threat of indulgence. Ponderously Thurber marshals the evidence to show how sensitive writers have had to change their story line to satisfy audience and advertiser demand (some reviewers objected to the inclusion of "Soapland" in *The Beast in Me* on the grounds that it was boring). Sadly he shows how the drama indulges its audience's most commonplace desires. Yet it is precisely on these two ideas that Thurber builds the comedy of Walter Mitty and Kinstrey in "The Whip-Poor-Will." At best,

"Soapland" gives its audience "simplicity, honesty, and warm belief in common humanity." The comic enemy in the modern world, however, is Mrs. Mitty, or the editor in "The Waters of the Moon," people who say that life is simple, that man has acquired honesty, that common humanity is warm and satisfying. Usually in "Soapland," Thurber says, the "sun is. . .directly overhead, casting a steady and monotonous glare, unrelieved by the subtlety of shadows." Such a landscape is clear, but the light is not true to human experience. "Soapland" is full of base wisdom but it has none of the noble folly.

The unity of *The Beast in Me* derives from the desire of Thurber's mind for complexity and richness as contrasted to the reduction and simplification of "Soapland." The aim—to examine the conventional with fresh insight—appears in "Here Come the Tigers," a story about two slightly drunken friends who appear at the narrator's house late at night with a mad scheme to evolve "a new dimension of meaning. . .And a new plane of beauty." Their discovery is that rearranging the letters of a given word produces new words that reflect the character or tone of the original word. Thus they delightfully find that the letters of *stiff* also spell *fist, tiff,* and *fits.* They accuse the narrator, who is not charmed, of "The obscurantism of the explicit." Even if he is not charmed, he is hooked by the idea and he spends a sleepless night after they leave trying to discover the three other words that can be spelled with *tiger.* Exploring the complexity of the human mind is the very soul of modern comedy since in working our way out of complexity we sense the human triumph.

Two stories in *The Beast in Me,* in which the various directions of the book reach a focus, state most fully the search for and delight in complexity. Both of these stories owe much to Henry James. The first, "A Call on Mrs. Forrester," carries a note under its title informing the reader that it was written "After rereading, in my middle years, Willa Cather's 'A Lost Lady' and Henry James's 'The Ambassadors.'" In "A Call on Mrs. Forrester" the narrator stands on a bridge below Mrs. Forrester's house in a town "somewhere between Omaha and Denver." In the fashion of The Master, Thurber's narrator imagines a scene that will take place when he goes to the house, but he never makes the call. He refuses to visit the woman because the charm of James's Madame de Vionnet (the heroine in *The Ambassadors*) is stronger than that of the earthy, vigorous, lying Mrs. Forrester. Mrs. Forrester is so very familiar to the reader that she must be a significant American archetype, a reflection of national character. Like Mrs. Kinstrey in "The Whip-Poor-Will," she is not at all funny. She is vulgar, stupid, unsavory; she responds only when she is worshipped. She is a travesty, a very uncomic Mrs. Mitty. She is to the United States what Mme. Bovary is to France. Her cluttered house is like the American landscape; her inability to remember anything and her propensity to be jealous of all things is the American barbarism which makes us sometimes so uncivilized and demanding. She would adore the radio dramas with their "steady and monotonous glare." On the other hand, Madame de Vionnet is a woman of whom it "was once said. . .that when she touched a thing the ugliness, God knows how, went out of it." The narrator prefers the beauty of Madame de Vionnet's world to the energy and ramshackle clutter of Mrs. Forrester's. The Frenchwoman has complexity, charm, civilization, the light and shadow that Willa Cather's woman lacks. She has the same noble folly which makes Mitty so funny.

Thurber's full scale parody of Henry James, "The Beast in the Dingle," also pits the apparently simple, honest, direct against the hero's preference for complexity, shadow, and beauty. In the story Charles Grantham, the hero, and Amy Lighter (as in James the names are wonderfully chosen) elaborately discuss an "interesting situation" reported by a lady in brown who has two children and two servants. The lady in brown fears the servants have some supernatural control over her children. At the end of the story Miss Lighter has thrown her light all over the lovely little mystery only to discover that the beast is nothing at all. The lady fabricated the mystery for cocktail party entertainment. Miss Lighter therefore concludes that their "situation" ends not with a whimper but with a bang.

Grantham has another interpretation. First he suspects that he is "the very type and sign of old J. Alfred Prufrock." He has taken his clue from Miss Lighter's quotation from Eliot, but the familiar situation changes in Thurber's story. Grantham continues to speak (note the rhythmic language):

If I should strike. . .at every rustling in the undergrowth, a high heroic stance, sword drawn from cane, and cry, "Come out, come out!" and if there should advance in answer to my challenge, on veritable tippy-toe, the most comical of beasts, about its neck a pink and satiny ribbon tied in the fluffiest of bows, what, dear lady, in the name of Heaven would become of me? Well, there it was, then, his beast in the dingle, out in the open at last, scampering about, and when she could find breath, Miss Lighter, merrily laughing, put a name to it. "A kitty cat," she cried, "a kitty cat for a tiger!"

"Oh," said Grantham, "for the matter of that, a bunny rabbit."

"But isn't that precisely what *I*, cocktail in hand, challenged from the bushes?" his friend gaily demanded.

"Oh, but you *challenged* it," he threw back at her, "while I watched, from a safe and sorry distance." He brought out, before she could prevent it, an epitaph. "Here lies one who tippy-toed away from it, away from you, away from *us*."

But Grantham's tippy-toeing is the comic strut of a man leaving a monster; or in comic terms, he is a man escaping from the threat of Amy Lighter's dull, prosaic light just as Mitty escaped. In the comic world, Thurber makes the same point that "Soapland" makes.

Although Thurber parodies James's style, he does not repeat James's theme in *The Beast in the Jungle.* In James's story, a man has not had the courage to live; in Thurber's story a man refuses to accept the "sun. . .directly overhead, casting a steady and monotonous glare, unrelieved by the subtlety of shadows." Thurber's character goes tippy-toeing off with "shoulders squared, head erect." Although the James character is defeated, Thurber's character triumphs. As with Mitty, the triumph is lonely; Grantham refuses Miss Lighter's offer to marry him and leaves the country on a diplomatic mission. He prefers the shadow and scorns the lady who pries, arriving at the same dull, prosaic fact that Mrs. Mitty, Mrs. Kinstrey, and Thurber's other female impostors know. Thus, at the end of "The Beast in the Dingle," the reader perceives the unifying idea of the whole collection: a useful and beautiful delusion is better than a discovered fact or a supposed fact. Since mind alone creates meaning, then rich and significant meaning is preferable to the kitty cat that Miss Lighter finds.

In the history of comedy, the comic plot results when a hero, who represents to his audience the possibilities of birth and growth and fertility, defeats the challenge of an impostor. In ancient times the hero wears the mask of a new god and the impostor is the god of the old year who must be destroyed. In later comedy the impostor is a pedant, a bragging soldier, a father who prevents the young man from marrying the girl. The basic pattern in Thurber is the same, but the oppressive element changes. The oppressive element is that kind of mind which prevents the hero from living the rich, full, and deliberate life. Oppression may come in the comfort of Mrs. Walter Mitty. It may come in the insensitiveness of Mrs. Kinstrey, the wife in "The Whip-Poor-Will." It may come in the mindless repetition of formulae by Mrs. Ulgine Barrows in "The Catbird Seat." It may come in the super-patriot of the era of McCarthyism, or it may come from the facile generalizations of the editor in "The Waters of the Moon." Or, it may come from Amy Lighter's penetrating the mystery of the lady in brown. These threats do not destroy life (as they threaten to in the old comedy); rather they seek to destroy the meaningful understanding of life.

The meaningful understanding of life is the life we feel in Thurber's heroes: the life of the heroic imagination of Walter Mitty, of the redeemed society of F & S where Erwin Martin heads the filing department. It is the world where insensitivity is destroyed (as in "The Whip-Poor-Will"). It is the world of Thurber's own inventive resurgences in "The Waters of the Moon." Negatively, this rich life is that which is not found in "Soapland" except in the case of a few writers of radio scripts who have tried, futilely, to inject the human experience into the form. It is the world of intelligent, civilized, thinking response that Charles Grantham prefers to Miss Amy Lighter's neat explanation. It is Madame de Vionnet.

It is not a clearly defined ideal. Thurber is not a moralist nor a rational philosopher reducing life to a pattern of meaning. He is an artist presenting, as completely and fully as he can, a comic vision of experience. We know that vision and its meanings when we know the characters who have it. We do not reduce them to a series of axioms for behavior, but we are fed and enriched by the victory which each of them experiences over the impostor of the corpulent, insensitive modern world.

In utilizing the threat of mind against his comic heroes, Thurber attaches his comedy to a major perception of our philosophy. Loren Eiseley writes,

> From the oscillating universe beating like a gigantic heart, to the puzzling existence of antimatter, order, in a human sense, is at least partially an illusion. Ours, in reality, is the order of a time, and of an insignificant fraction of the cosmos, seen by the limited sense of a finite creature. . . . We are more dangerous than we seem and more potent in our ability to materialize an unexpected [universe] which is drawn from our minds. (*American Scholar*, XXXV (1965), 428)

In that statement I see Walter Mitty with his illusion of order and Kinstrey in his cry for order and human understanding. Amy Lighter is dangerous, as Eiseley uses the word, for she converts an illusion of order into a fact. Eiseley's desperate situation becomes magically transformed in Thurber into a subject for laughter and comedy. His heroes are the men who can conceive of a larger order than a simple formula, than the simple sun, who can remain in the moonlit marges of the mind. His comedy is, therefore, a powerful release and pleasure.

VI

The Comedy
of Ritual Bondage: The Fables

In addition to sketches and short stories, Thurber also wrote
in his "high middle period" *Fables for Our Time* (1940) and *Further
Fables for Our Time* (1956). Although the second collection stands
outside the period, its tone resembles that found in the work of
the 1940's.* The method is the same as in the Henry James parodies, but in the fables the method is even richer and more satisfying.
In the fables Thurber adopts the tradition of Aesop, La Fontaine,
and other folk writers to speak about his own time, and the reader
laughs at the incongruity of our experience written in fable style.
Thurber is rigidly bound to a quirk; he is a Druid priest repeating
arcane formulae that magically communicate our experience. We
expect nonsense but we find sense.

His method is extremely dangerous since any third-rate writer
can repeat ritual for laughs. George Ade's *Fables in Slang* employ
the same technique that Thurber uses, but his results are often
disastrous; his formula of retelling folk stories in slang attracts
so much attention to itself that the reader looks at the method more
than the statement or any possible reason for telling the stories in
such a manner. Because the method leans so close to the trite and
trivial, Thurber's success in avoiding either triteness or triviality
truly satisfies the reader. In an astonishing number of fables,

*The second collection is superior, I suspect, because of the advance in vision gained
in writing the stories for children, *Many Moons, The Great Quillow, The White Deer* and
The Thirteen Clocks. The next chapter discusses these important stories.

Thurber makes the fable communicate so naturally that his meaning and his method are one, each contributing to the other.

The fables employ a standard comic technique of repeating a habit or custom beyond what is appropriate to the situation. Of all Thurber's work, the fables require the reader to remember that they first appeared amidst the *New Yorker's* whiskey, perfume, and jewelry advertisements. Amidst the affluence, they are as incongruous as a nineteenth-century costume at a cocktail party. Published outside of the *New Yorker,* the fables use Thurber's drawings (the drawings in the second collection are all old drawings) to establish twentieth-century urban values. The fables are funny, therefore, for the same reason that a long nose is funny. Henri Bergson, who defines this *leitmotif* of comedy, says that a long nose is funny because the soul is caught in a habit of noseness and does not know to stop. Thurber is caught in a bondage of fable-ness and does not know when to stop. Or, in more formal language, Bergson defines his *leitmotif* as a "lack of elasticity. . . when the circumstances of the case called for something else." (See *Works Consulted*) The movie-cartoon character taking several steps in thin air before discovering that he has walked over the edge of a cliff illustrates the same lack of elasticity. When Thurber writes fables, he continues a form which seems not what the circumstances of the glossy advertisements or the urbane cartoons call for. He behaves eccentrically or inelastically. We are surprised just as we would be surprised upon seeing a man in a Prince Albert coat in the purlieus of Park Avenue. We are even more surprised if we discover that the coat is not an accidental costume but that the wearer has some logical or illogical reason for wearing it. The habit of fable-ness becomes, in effect, another mask.

In borrowing a form, Thurber advances the dimension of his comedy: he is not only comic by language and vision but by method or style. Previously he used forms that have nothing inherently comic in them. He writes comic essays, comic autobiography, or comic short stories. With the fables, however, he has not only his familiar subjects for comic treatment but also a style that is comic, for with the mask of Aesop (and all his imitators), he acquires a pattern or design which he can further exploit for comedy. It follows that since he has a set form in his new comic mask, he has, paradoxically, more freedom to use his language and vision. He

rides on the shoulders of Aesop and La Fontaine just as the
Renaissance painter rode on the shoulders of his apprentices when
he gave them the task of detail work so that he might concentrate
on the essential vision of the painting. Thurber is thus freer because his entire creative effort is devoted to achieving his final
effect. He does not have to invent a language. An examination of
his fables shows (a) how Thurber uses the fable as a comic mask,
(b) how he uses the technique of continuation to obtain his comedy
and his statement, and (c) how the form invites the reader to assume a position of superiority which comedy requires.

The Fable as Comic Form

Using the fable mask, Thurber writes succinctly, directly and
concretely about human vanity, human credulity, and human
carelessness. He can even discuss politics. As I have noted in the
earlier discussions of the comic mask, the form gives him distance
so that he can talk about the impassioned upheavals of our sorry
time. He is, of course, no less involved because of the grace and
gentleness of his art, but he speaks more forcefully with his grace
and gentleness. He wrote these fables just before the Second World
War and during the cold war, a time when an artist might forget
his art for the sake of propaganda. Thurber, however, develops
into a more complete artist in the form. He uses more starkly and
clearly the comic plot. The irony of the fable permits a deeper
and more profound statement about the human condition. Thus in
the fable we find the paradox of the natural (the seemingly right
and proper) merged with the artistic (the seemingly deliberate and
artificial).

Thurber successfully transcribes calamity in comic form when
he is freed from literal truth and literal motivation. "The Green
Isle in the Sea," for example, published in *Fables for Our Time,*
tells about a little old gentleman who goes out to enjoy a bright
sunny morning. The world rebuffs him at every turn. A spider
narrowly misses poisoning him as he enjoys the sun on his bal-
cony; a small boy pulls a chair out from under him at breakfast;
a child's hoop trips him as he walks on the sidewalk; a robber
steals his watch, his money, "and a gold ring his mother had given
him when he was a boy."

When at last the old gentleman staggered into the little park, which had been to him a fountain and a shrine, he saw that half the trees had been killed by a blight, and the other half by a bug. Their leaves were gone and they no longer afforded any protection from the skies, so that the hundred planes which appreared suddenly overhead had an excellent view of the little old gentleman through their bombing sights.

To say that Man is defenseless requires a novelist hundreds of pages. In the novel we need to know the hero's name, his origin, and the state of his innocence. We need to know all the possible gossip connected with the real man. The gossip may be interesting, but it is more likely the trivia necessary to sustain our willing suspension of disbelief. What war, what planes, or what blight is irrelevant to Thurber's point about the fragility of life in an improbable and impossible universe where the greatest fear is man himself. In the fable Thurber strips away the inessential, stripping away even himself, to focus on fragility. Thus paring the subject to its essentials, Thurber gives his subject the full brunt of his language power. The fable is a kind of lyric poem in which the variation of the form, the grace, and the gentleness are fully realized.

Within the form of the fable, the reader sees more starkly and clearly the familiar comic plot. We sense plainly and directly the comic struggle between the old villain and the quick, young hero. Freed from the minutiae of realistic characters, the fables concentrate fully on the ancient and typical pattern of comedy. As usual, Thurber adjusts the endings to suit his ironic vision. "The Two Turkeys" in the first collection speaks in the ironic tone familiar in the 1930's in which Thurber's young and vigorous hero is swept away before he can establish the new society that comedy and comic characters aim to establish. An old turkey who has "been cock of the walk for many years" prepares to meet the challenge of a young turkey who boasts that he will "knock that old buzzard cold one of these days." Just when the two are squared away for the familiar contest, a farmer sweeps up the young turkey and wrings his neck. The moral of the fable is that "Youth will be served, frequently stuffed with chestnuts." We are back in the familiar world of "Destructive Forces in Life" (*Let Your Mind Alone*). The turkey is swept off by a *deus ex machina* that brings no benefit or ease just as Harry Connor is defeated by his practical-

joker of a friend, Bert Scursey. Connor leaves his home in New
York to live in Oregon. Like the ironic endings which leave characters with little hope, the turkey is carried off to destruction. Both
stories speak of modern man's inability to order life toward any
triumph, but the fable conveys its idea more swiftly and more
comically.

The same comic plot in the second collection of fables, however, frequently gives the hero a touch of a final victory. In "The
Sea and the Shore," the first of the *Further Fables for Our Time,*
two primordial creatures ooze out of the sea onto the land. The
female, as we expect in Thurber, has more energy than the male.
She "prefigured mistily things that would one day become rose-
point lace and taffeta, sweet perfumes and jewelry." The male
returns to the sea, but "A couple of eons later, the male, unable
to get along alone, reappeared one day upon the shore." The vital
surge within him triumphs in "a mindless urge deep inside him
[that] took on the frail flicker of desire." Far away in the distance
we hear the hymn that ends the Greek comedy. In the parallel
fable at the end of the collection, with the reversed title "The Shore
and the Sea," a scholarly lemming watches a stampede of lemmings back into the sea and tears up "what he had written through
the years about his species, and started his studies all over again."
In neither version does Thurber bring forward the full triumphant
marriage feast of the old comedy, but at least there is in both a
"frail flicker" of joy. If the species seems doomed to destruction,
one lemming and one man have the energy to start all over again.
These fables are genuinely mythic, then, incorporating the cosmic
action of man and his experience in simple, direct figures.

"The Cat in the Lifeboat" in *Further Fables for Our Time*
gathers a rich, wise and serious yield from the comic plot. The
plot is stark. The impostor is a cat named William and the hero
is a cat on a remote island who defeats him. Like a cat, William
is impervious to the world around him; he "came to believe that
he was the Will of Last Will and Testament, and the Willy of Willy
Nilly, and the cat who put the cat in the catnip. He finally became
convinced that Cadillacs were Catillacs because of him." A cat-
crazy woman is so impressed with William's "Tall tales of his
mythical exploits, honors, blue ribbons, silver cups, and medals"
that she decides to take him on a trip around the world. Unfor-

tunately when their ship sinks, William is unceremoniously tossed out of the lifeboat, "like a long incompleted forward pass." Although he swims until he reaches "the sullen shore of a sombre island inhabited by surly tigers, lions, and other great cats," he suffers from "traumatic amnesia" and cannot remember who he is or where he came from. The great cats on the island call him Nobody from Nowhere. He loses "his ninth life in a barroom brawl with a young panther who had asked him what his name was and where he came from and got what he considered an uncivil answer." He is buried in an unmarked grave. Thurber's moral is "O why should the spirit of mortal be proud, in this little voyage from swaddle to shroud?" Thus the comic plot is fully presented. The impostor, the cat who thought he was so important, meets the young comic hero in the cats on the distant island and is defeated. At the end we celebrate the victory of the island cats who destroyed William, the impostor.

No description or summary can communicate the meaning of "The Cat in the Lifeboat"; the fable is more than its parts. We laugh at the egotistical cat, we recognize the correspondence between cats and humans, and we accept the moral as an appropriate resolution of the comic plot. With the utmost economy Thurber presents the cat's pride and defeat. The fable offers the familiar idea of vanity in a different way; thus the idea takes on new life and makes a fresh appeal to our understanding. The idea of vanity has been often thought but never so well expressed. Or, to say it another way, the fable makes us see an idea so familiar that we had forgotten its meaning until the fable dramatized it once more. Thurber's fable is, consequently, a mythic and comic statement about the human condition.

The mythic or comic tone of these fables is extremely stylized. It is unnatural, in one sense, although no one would object to the simple and stark movement. But we are also delighted because Thurber moves so gracefully and gently in the form that, paradoxically, his expression seems natural and his adaptation or changes seem natural. Consider, for example, the first fable in his first collection, "The Mouse Who Went to the Country." Aesop's original is simplicity itself (and has been imitated by writers from Sir Thomas Wyatt through Jean de La Fontaine and Marianne Moore). In Aesop (and many old versions) the city mouse disdain-

fully accepts country fare and then takes the country mouse back
to dine on delicacies in the city. Ravenous cats attack them. The
moral is that the grass is not greener on the other side of the fence.
Another implicit moral is that life away from the trauma of city
life is worth the lack of luxury: eat dull country food and know
dull country pleasures but also avoid hungry cats. Thurber has
another variation to play. In his version, called "The Mouse Who
Went to the Country," the poor city mouse gets so involved in
commuter schedules that he never arrives in the country. After
taking the wrong bus, he walks home to the city. The moral is the
same — Thurber says, "Stay where you are, you're sitting pretty" —
but the idea differs: the trauma of Aesop's city has spread now to
the countryside. In Aesop there is safety in the country, but in
Thurber there is safety nowhere. We do not fear monsters; we
fear imperfectly organized schedules. The older versions had a
triumph since the country mouse goes home to his rough fare
happily, but in Thurber's version the miasma is impossible to
avoid. Thurber wrote other versions of the same fable in "The
Mouse and the Money" and "The Bat Who Got the Hell Out." In
the story of the Bat, Thurber exploits the fable idea of following
one's inherent character to make a comment on man's inability to
find, know, or follow his own inherent character. The fable tells
of a Bat who decided life would be more pleasant as a human
being because humans go to heaven when they die. Like the country mouse, he leaves his bat warren and goes to the city of humans,
to arrive just when a best-selling evangelist is "dragging God down
to the people's level." The Bat returns to his warren because, "By
decent minds is he abhorred who'd make a Babbitt of the Lord."
In these fables the form becomes a metaphor, an enlightening
comparison between humans and animals that condemns human
depravity and vulgarity in the story of the bat, or projects human
difficulties in the version of the City Mouse and the Country Mouse.
Uniting old stories with new experience Thurber obtains meanings
larger than the mere events or characters described.

In addition, Thurber uses the fable as a skeleton for rhetorical
play. He is not the first to do so; the educational system of Greece
required students to practice rhetoric by retelling fables. Thurber's
are a storehouse of rhetorical devices, often used so subtly and
easily that pointing them out destroys them. I also hesitate to point

them out because I remember "Here Lies Miss Groby," a sketch about a teacher who preferred counting devices in literature to reading it (*My World*). "The Human Being and the Dinosaur" contains a "flyteing," a ceremonial vilification: the human declares to the dinosaur, "You are all wrong in the crotch, and in the cranium, and in the cortex." In the following sentence, he balances triads (the three verbs) with three nouns: "He sat loose, sang pretty, and slept tight, in a hundred honey locusts and cherry trees and lilac bushes." Sentences prick and play with memory since the fables, like other modern works, are a museum of quotations and arcane bits of information. Like the rhetorical devices, the quotations and allusions are kept well subservient to the fable meaning. A sentence in "The Turtle Who Conquered Time," reads, "The sounds of jubilee were no longer heard in the once merry meadow, and the summer seemed to languish like a dying swan." The sentence repeats the lilting melody of Tennyson's "And after many a summer dies the swan." The quotation from "Tithonus" is apt, for Tennyson's poem, like "The Turtle Who Conquered Time," dramatizes the terrible awareness of fact in contrast with human desire. The echo of Tennyson's line lends its grace to reinforce the fable. Examples of such language play are legion, but pulled out of the context of the stories they do not give the pleasure of discovery that the reader should feel when he finds them. No matter how alert the reader, he is unlikely to catch them all and so he keeps coming back to look for more.

The language of the fables, although it never departs from prose, is sometimes as full of rhyme, rhythm, and ritual as the most mysterious incantation. "The Truth about Toads" begins with ceremonial statements from various creatures about their own importance. Each statement is a cliché transformed: " 'I am the real Macaw,' squawked the Macaw proudly." A Marlin says, "You should have seen the one I got away from." The energy of these variations is marvelous. The moral tag at the end of each fable often rhymes; sometimes the rhyme deliberately hits with all the misdirected strength of doggerel, but sometimes the lines end in off-rhymes that nag at the expectations. One moral reads, "She who goes unarmed in Paradise should first be sure that's where she is." The *paradise: where-she-is* rhyme is both close enough to and far enough from true rhyme to give the statement force. The

most lovely of these morals ends the fable of "The Turtle Who
Conquered Time"; "Oh, why should the shattermyth have to be a
crumplehope and a dampenglee?" Granted one could say approxi-
mately the same in "Facts make people unhappy," but the prosaic
statement utterly lacks the passion of Thurber's language.

Leafing through the pages of either collection of fables, the
reader is constantly struck by the felicitous use of balance and
antithesis, of allusions, of rhyme and rhythm. They do not offend
the reader because they are appropriate to the naive, primitive
fable; in fact they delight the reader because of the triumph in our
surprise of recognition.

The surprise of recognition comes also—with one final way in
which Thurber exploits his form—when we discover the irony of
his statement. In our sophisticated, and thus jaded, time, the form
reawakens our sense of wonder so that we can detect a new discovery or revelation. Both the riddle and the fable are the oldest
forms of writing that we have preserved and both demand that the
reader be surprised by their resolution or their moral. Since we
try to anticipate, the form invites us to read for meaning which is
beyond the apparent. When the reader is prepared to read beyond
the words, then he is ready to expect irony. Though the fables are
about animals, we are not reading them for the animal story but for
the animal's representation of human qualities. Irony is a persistent and pertinacious quality of all of Thurber's prose, but it is
even more evident in the fables. Because of their economy and com-
pactness, the irony is both more apparent and more persuasive.

The early fables use obvious irony; the moral to the new version
of "The Little Girl and the Wolf" in *Fables for Our Time* says, "It
is not so easy to fool little girls nowadays as it used to be." We
readily see the irony of changing the wolf of the old story into a
predatory male. "The Tiger Who Understood People," also in the
first collection, is more subtle. In this fable a tiger decides to imi-
tate humans in staging a fixed prize fight. Although the tiger and
the leopard "boxers" inaugurate a full public relations program,
the animals of the jungle are too wise to pay the admission price
of a wild boar carcass that the tiger expects. And so the tiger and
the leopard, weak from lack of food, are easy prey for the "couple
of wild boars who come wandering along." On the one hand we

are invited to praise the tiger for his ingenuity, but on the other we discover a stupidity which only the human possesses. The moral is a low-keyed statement: "If you live as humans do, it will be the end of you." If an animal ascends the scale of intelligence, he violates his own habitual patterns of action and thus destroys himself. The fable does not say explicitly that Man is stupid, but a reader could hardly understand anything else. The fable thus meets a basic definition of irony, a way of speaking that means more than what it says.

The fables are also ironic in another way. The ironic mode uses characters who exhibit a power of action inferior to the one assumed to be normal or a mode in which the writer's attitude is one of detached objectivity. The definition describes the fable. We are superior to the animals and to the human beings who appear; our attitude toward them is one of detached objectivity. In "The Father and His Daughter" a parent lectures his child on the necessity of the daughter's giving away some of her birthday books to a nice little neighbor boy. A few weeks later, however, when the father goes to his library to look up the word *father* in the *Oxford English Dictionary,* he discovers that his daughter has given away four of the thirteen volumes. The superior father is demonstrating an action inferior to the one assumed to be normal; he "thought he was a philosopher and a child psychologist, and couldn't shut his big fatuous mouth," Thurber writes. The animals in "The Tiger Who Understood People" see through the hoax of a staged prize fight and see through the vain boasts of the tiger and the leopard. Mankind does not see through propaganda usually; thus the animals are, although apparently inferior, in fact superior.

A further kind of largeness is the ironic discovery of the truth of Thurber's fables. In Thurber's seemingly simple fables of real animals, we discern life as a sacrament; pride and vanity are the pantheon. The hero of "The Cat and the Lifeboat" suffers as Oedipus suffers for his vanity; the moth in "The Clothes Moth and the Luna Moth" has the passion of Helen; the squirrel in "The Turtle Who Conquered Time" gives us the bittersweet knowledge of Hermes. And in a fable like "The Peacelike Mongoose," the story of a creature who was accused of being "mongoosexual," we see a pattern of events in our time raised to mythic size. "The

Tiger Who Understood People" and "The Cat in the Lifeboat" repeat the old story of the fall of man. The artist thus makes clear for us the universal aspect of humanity; his simple animal stories re-enact the old struggles that have attracted men since the dawn of awareness.

The fables expand into human experience. If the fables are read as pretty little variations on familiar ideas, we are missing their point. They re-enact events that are beyond human will. Because they are stripped down to bare essentials, Thurber achieves a comedy of complete concentration. With his bare materials, he has a form upon which he can use his artistry, his metaphors, his rhetorical devices, and his symbols. Because of the concentration, he is at the heart of the matter. To attract the attention of a reader again is the mark of a superior artist using his form to communicate significant understanding.

The Familiar Habit and Statement

The fable is a form which writers have used to teach from time immemorial. It is closely related to the parable in its effort to judge human experience and correct behavior. Our literary fashions, however, do not approve of blunt judgment about experience. We want our morals implicit in the material rather than overtly stated. If Thurber opts for a form which allows a moral, he must be extremely sure that attention is on the wit of the handling rather than on the lesson in the fable. One obvious way to effect this wit is to tell a story with a moral which is not the one intended. In the disjuncture between the apparent statement and the apparent meaning, Thurber leaves an entry through which the reader will intuit a real meaning. "The Sheep in Wolf's Clothing" in the first collection of fables tells about two sheep who put on wolf's clothing to spy in Wolfland. Since they arrive in Wolfland on a holiday, each spy concludes "Wolves are just like us, for they gambol and frisk. Every day is fete day in Wolfland." Each sneaks off to write a book recording his observation, but rather than checking his evidence each labors to get his book before the public first. The sheep believe the stories, withdraw their sentinels, and the wolves attack, "howling and slavering," and kill the sheep as easy "as flies on a windowpane." The moral is "Don't get it right, just get it written." The moral is appropriate, but the moral misses the crux of the story. We are delighted, as readers, that indirection seems to find direction out, and we are delighted that Thurber can go against the rule ("Fiction cannot make direct judgments about the affairs of society") and yet not violate the rule. The actual moral, that our society pays a premium for favorable reports, is off to one side, so to speak, where the reader can grasp it himself. The statement, however, is made.

An obvious need is to keep the reader always ready to accept the surface values in the story so that he will accept the possibility of the surface moral. When Thurber recasts an old fable, he has available the familiar pattern against which he can counterpose his new statement. He has a little more difficulty (and therefore more potential pleasure) when he makes his own fable. In "The Lion Who Wanted to Zoom," "The Scotty Who Knew Too Much," and "The Crow and the Oriole" he takes the familiar attitude of the fabulist telling stories about animals attempting to deny their own nature by changing into some other creature. Aesop's "The Jackdaw Who Would Be an Eagle" tells of such an attempted transformation, but Thurber cannot rely on the old story in his new version since he adds contemporary details. The Lion, for example, hoodwinks an eagle out of his wings, but when the Lion tries to fly he crashes into a rock and bursts "into flames." The detail suggests photographs of crashing airplanes. The Eagle then puts on the Lion's mane and goes home to his nervous wife who shoots him dead with a pistol she keeps in her "bureau drawer." The stated moral is that one should never allow a nervous female to own a pistol. Again the stated moral is off on a quite different tangent from the actual understood moral. The Scotty story describes a city dog who attacks a skunk and a porcupine and is twice defeated, but then tries to use his newly gained knowledge from these battles to fight the farm dogs: he attacks with one paw holding his nose and the other paw held to parry the knives he thinks the porcupine had used. The farm dogs have a holiday. The Crow divorces his crow wife in confident expectation of a happy life with a complaisant Baltimore oriole; when he returns to his crow wife, he finds a message advising him that she has found a new mate and that there is some arsenic in the medicine chest. The basic fable lesson — consider the facts before find-

ing a conclusion — is stated explicitly only in the story of the Crow
and in that fable the moral seems detached from the story: "Even
the llama should stick to mamma." In this moral, however, the
indirection is seemingly more apparent than the direction and our
attention is directed toward the wit which allows us to see, almost
unconsciously, the true lesson.

If he sometimes inverts his story to run counter to his moral,
Thurber will also audaciously attach an explicit moral to a story
drawn directly from the newspapers. "The Very Proper Gander"
could be described as an animal version of the suspicion and fear
so often visible in American politics. The Gander of the title is a
very exemplary citizen who sings to his wife and children. When
another creature remarks that he is "a very proper gander," an old
hen misinterprets the remark as being something about *propaganda.*
Another hen, a duck, and a guinea hen magnify the story and set
upon the gander, driving him out of the country. The moral is quite
explicit: "Anybody who you or your wife thinks is going to overthrow the government by violence must be driven out of the country."
In this case, Thurber violates our expectation by exercising his wit
on the way of representing fear and suspicion in the barnyard.
His comedy is his revealing device rather than the statement, and
the comedy dominates the actual or the apparent content by its
version of familiar events.

The requirement is that we must always feel the springing
invention of comic wit which, we confidently expect, will expose
another facet of folly, complexity, or delusion in our experience.
The first collection of fables is not as free to discover, invent, or
reveal as the second collection, *Further Fables for Our Time.* While
the first collection is content to retell the familiar, the second collection energetically recasts contemporary experience into the fable
mold. He writes five new versions of "The Fox and the Crow." He
transforms our mania for speed into a new fable called "The Wolf
Who Went Places." This wolf, rich and secure, goes around the
world in practically no time and meets "a speed-crazy young wolf-
ess, with built-in instantaneous pickup ability," but the two are
killed trying "to turn in to Central Park from Fifth Avenue while
traveling at the rate of 175 miles an hour, watching television, and
holding hands." In "The Cricket and the Wren" the Wren helps
the Cricket judge a singing contest by performing various helpful

services. When the Cricket, not unnaturally, awards the singing prize to the very helpful Wren, the Wren nobly spirits the Cricket out of town ahead of a raging mob of disappointed contestants. In both fables, the reader's pleasure comes from seeing how the fabulist makes speed and log-rolling, contemporary manifestations of folly and delusion, serve his own wit. "The Wolf Who Went Places" and "The Cricket and the Wren" illustrate Thurber's power to use an ancient method to make his own statement. He catches the rhythm of the fabulist but uses and invests the rhythm with fresh insight.

To deduce from these fables any political or social statement is dangerous, and yet they seem clearly to invite just that. The reader senses a Divine Justice that destroys speed-crazy young wolves, but the reader also wryly notes that Wrens do subvert the free play of talent in singing contests. The fables advocate cautious, careful examination of facts since the characters they describe are destroyed because they give in to folly or delusion. As expected in an old form, the fables condemn hens who turn a sentence like "He is a very proper gander" into something about propaganda; the failure of human equipment is as much a *leitmotif* as the fable method itself. The characters in his fables are caught in their habits as Thurber is caught in his habit of writing fables.

If the fables make statements about politics and social behavior, Thurber also uses the method to make his readers aware of mutability, beauty, and value. We discover the beauty and the value in the very excitement of his language. "Oh, why should the shattermyth have to be a crumplehope and a dampenglee?" a moral exclaims and charms us (the lyricism is balanced by a vulgar story of a grasshopper making a profit out of a turtle with a date on its back). The moral of "The Clothes Moth and the Luna Moth" has none of the lilting melody of the moral above—but this fable dramatizes the frantic energy of desire so lyrically that the prosaic, harsh moral is needed to establish the juxtaposition between method and statement that marks the fables. The Luna Moth in the fable calls the Clothes Moth "a mulch. . .a mulbus, a crawg, and a common creeb," but the Clothes Moth persists in his desire. He strikes so repeatedly at the window pane that separates him from the Luna that he finally manages to make a small opening. The Clothes Moth dies, but the Luna "flew swiftly and gracefully toward the candle on the mantelpiece and was consumed in its flame with a little zishing sound like that made by a lighted cigarette dropped in a cup of coffee." In this, and in other fables, the persistence of desire, the precariousness of beauty, and the fragility of life are celebrated in a form which seems to provide other pleasures. Giving these graceful fables any ponderous meaning takes away from their ease, but they create a new awareness of transitory life and suggest values. In the dimension of the fables, almost anything seems possible, for they balance the impulse to statement with their detachment to allow a reader's perception of meaning beyond what paraphrase or summary can suggest. The fable form permits Thurber to speak about such basic ideas of his civilization as the use of intelligence and the concept of imagination. Philip Rahv in a 1940 essay, "The Cult of Experience in American Writing" (it appeared first in the *Partisan Review* and is reprinted in Morton Zabel's *Literary Opinion in America)* isolates a characteristic thirst for sensation to the exclusion of ideas in most American writing. We distrust ideas; in addition to our literature, our politics is marked by an insistent pragmatism. How Thurber differs in these fables from his contemporaries Faulkner, Hemingway, or Fitzgerald! They give us the sensation, a felt life almost devoid of ideas. They distrust ideas as mere delusions. Thurber, on the other hand, keeps the sensation in his style; he dares to use his style to make us understand ideas.

The Superior Position of the Reader

Possibly the humanist has lost some of his authority because he invariably speaks from a position of a superior observer of the human condition. Clutching his values to his breast, he advances in the world giving only fitful views of his precious commodity. In comedy, however, the reader is superior to the stereotypes. The animal fable permits this superiority easily. We are all superior to dinosaurs, cats, foolish hens, ducks, or even the people who occasionally act out the fable. Whatever values these creatures may possess they are inferior to the reader or the comic audience in general; the comic audience has the delightful task of choosing from inferiors what he wants to take without the embarrassment of taking the golden thoughts of a preacher or a teacher. Because the animals repeat their animal behavior we know our superiority to them and their habits.

"A really living life," Bergson says, "should never repeat itself." When a man does repeat himself, he becomes funny. Eccentricity is a way of repeating oneself since the eccentric is, above all, a man whose behavior is predictably different. Mrs. Ulgine Barrows repeats her baseball clichés and we laugh at her repetition. With animals, however, we expect repetition, but since fable animals are quasi-human, we laugh at the animals as if they were humans caught in a bondage. Further, we seem to be reading the words of an unconscious Aesop of our time who doesn't realize that he is continuing like a machine and thus violating our ordinary experience which never repeats itself. So Thurber's imitation of Aesop takes the moralistic attitude of the fabulist and subjects it to the drubbing of the twentieth century. The reader is superior both to the animals who are caught and to the method of telling their story, and from our superior position we look down on the action without humiliation or self-abasement and see its value.

Parody is the natural voice for Thurber. His first book, *Is Sex Necessary?*, parodies (although sometimes it merely burlesques) the sexual self-help books of the liberated twenties. *The Owl in the Attic* mocks the tone and attitude of newspaper pet columnists and Fowler's dictionary of usage. *The Middle-Aged Man on the Flying Trapeze* prints "If Grant Had Been Drinking at Appomattox," a parody of a series of magazine articles appearing in *Scribner's Magazine.* In all of these illustrations (and there are more), the reader takes a position of superiority to laugh at the repetition of a custom or a habit, but the laughter is not just at the habit but is also a response to the statement.

The fables, or any other parody, mirror and enlarge their original. The fables amuse because they repeat antique stories or habits and thus we feel a position of superiority and disinterest as we look at the parody. We then grasp the mythic meaning, the universal statement about the human condition in the action. The fable form is the lever by which Thurber and his readers move the world. On the fulcrum of the comic plot, Thurber employs the artificial means which are his human powers: his sense of metaphor, symbol, and language. We sense the power that he applies and in the fable itself we see that power increased to its fullest potential. We "see through it" in that we know why the power has increased. Further, since the power is exerted on matters of significance—human vanity, behavior of massman, attempts to violate and even pervert human abilities, complexity, and beauty—the act attracts us. We "see through it" also, when we recognize that the man using the power is repeating a mode of behavior, that he is behaving inelastically when he tells fables, and we laugh with pleasure as we see him repeat his foolish habit. But at the same time that we realize his foolishness, we also appreciate his result: the foolishness isolates what is basic and essential to the human condition and gives it the harmony or repose of artistic form.

Thus the fables enter a tradition of American writing. We have the strange paradox of writing that seems to be done in a childish form yet succeeds in talking about very adult concerns. D. H. Lawrence in his *Studies in Classic American Literature* is fascinated that so much great American literature is known, and properly so, as boy's literature: *Huckleberry Finn, Moby Dick,* and even *The Scarlet Letter.* It always belies its appearance; behind its simple exterior lurk throbbing realities. I would give to a foreigner learning English these direct, graceful stories and know they would learn an English undefiled and find, at the same time, delight for the mind.

Because Thurber does not present five fables on vanity, five on warfare, five on beauty, or order his fables so that they strive at a single perception, the reader will get the greatest pleasure in reading *Fables for Our Time* and *Further Fables for Our Time* in small doses. The books are best kept close at hand so that one can read three or four fables in an odd moment and then absorb the experience. The fables support many rereadings so that the irony, the metaphors, and the consummate use of language become, for the moment, the focus of attention and pleasure. The second collection seems more consistently superior, but immediately on making the judgment, I remember "The Unicorn in the Garden" or "The Hen and the Heavens" (the sky did fall down when the hen said it was falling) in *Fables for Our Time.* In the less successful fables, attention goes to Thurber's cleverness in adapting the form; in the successful fable, the form reveals a facet of meaning in the story or in that aspect of the human condition that the story isolates.

The successful morals serve best when, like the final couplet of a Shakespearean sonnet, they both summarize and advance the perception of the fable. Sometimes the statement will be ridiculously inadequate and thus send the attention back to the fable. The moral to "The Hen and the Heavens" is the simple statement, "It wouldn't surprise me a bit if they did [fall]." Sometimes the moral will take the reader beyond the actual drama to make a specific application of the action; the moral for "The Tiger Who Understood People" is "If you live as humans do, it will be the end of you." The moral must surprise the reader just as the answer to a riddle surprises. The most successful morals surprise us continually because their rhythm and economy stick in the mind like aphorisms in a dramatic context. My favorite, the moral to "The Turtle Who Conquered Time"—"O why must a shattermyth be a crumplehope and dampenglee?"—is both simple and complex, what a child can see but only what an adult, practiced writer can say.

The moral, the form, the attitude, the technique are all worthy of praise in Thurber's fables. The fable is a dangerous but necessary way for an American to write. Thurber is quite worthy of comparison with the one other American fabulist, Marianne Moore. As he uses the form, its structure and design support his humanistic vision, his faith in ideas; and at the same time that he is interested in ideas, the fables themselves are sharp, concrete, and vivid. The fables organize our sensed experience and direct it toward thought. They inhabit the best part of two worlds.

VII

Incongruity:
Romances for Adults

In *The White Deer,* a knight-at-arms asks, "When all is dark within the house, who knows the monster from the mouse?" The question is typical: it contains both the incongruity of a knight worrying about a mouse that we expect of a comic writer but also the suggestion of wider meaning we expect from a writer of Romance. Like a Romancer, Thurber tells stories of knights and ladies, wizards and toymakers, and even of poets to make his most complete statement about the function of the imagination. He writes these books for the same reason that Sir Thomas Malory wrote his Romances of the Round Table. In both Thurber and Malory the action takes place on a human scale completely before the reader's eyes and yet the action refers to larger issues and larger scenes than what we actually see. As in Malory's Romances, the reader recognizes the hero's struggle with his enemies as a representative picture of civilization. Malory proposes the idea of *gentilesse* or *courtoisie* which allows his heroes to triumph; Thurber proposes the creative imagination. Both writers dramatize the particular quality they have chosen as the one thing necessary to preserve a dying civilization. The Romance, in both cases, concentrates on its own foreground, giving completely a world in which everything is immediate. In this world of Romance passions are acted out with pure objectivity to show that the comic incongruity of the stories is really a statement of utmost seriousness and importance.

The most obvious similarity between Malory's Romances and

Thurber's stories, however, is the violent times in which both writers lived. When he wrote about Arthur and his knights, Malory was in prison, England was being ravaged by the Wars of the Roses, and Europe by the plague. It was a period of discord and suffering. The Romance is, in fact, a kind of narrative that men write when they are overwhelmed by a world of brute force. In Malory's time it was gunpower: in Thurber's, nuclear fission. Malory lamented the decline in chivalry: Thurber inhabited a world which has hardly known a meaning for nobility. In the world of these stories beauty and truth might exist just as Malory re-creates French Romances where beauty and truth may exist in spite of the brute, naked, and paralyzing forces rampaging within his sight. As Thurber says in the "Foreword" to *The Thirteen Clocks,* "Unless modern Man wanders down these byways occasionally, I do not see how he can hope to preserve his sanity." *Escape* is the word that leaps to the reader's mind, but these stories are not an attempt at a permanent exit, they are a search for respite, a temporary flight from the pest house into courtly landscapes in which one might find balm for one's wounds and the strength and courage to re-enter the world of pain. Although the stories seem to exist in a never-never land, they recreate the pain of society in a pastoral world where the agony can be understood and where a remedy can be discovered and understood.

Thurber differs from Malory in his greater emphasis on comic incongruity. His stories laugh at the contrast between appearance and reality, while Malory was content to paint a gorgeous tapestry. A king who talks like Harold Ross, editor of the *New Yorker*, is funnier than Arthur modeled on Guy of Warwick. Saviors of society are not usually toymakers, villains do not really slay time. Thurber uses comic incongruity both for laughter and as part of his statement. Although we may laugh at a savior who is a toymaker, we also see that it is precisely his ability to make toys that permits him to triumph over the enemy of his society. The villains who slay time are in fact the archetype of a modern tendency that we abhor. Thurber then expands his vision beyond the vision in Malory by merging the methods of comic incongruity with the landscape of Romance.

Thurber published *Many Moons* in 1943. He followed it with *The Great Quillow* in 1944, *The White Deer* in 1945, *The Thirteen*

Clocks in 1950, and *The Wonderful O* in 1957. He does not call
them romances. He would undoubtedly be offended by an attempt
to name them something fancy. They can be read to children, but
they use the distant world of Romance and its ideals to comment
on the sterile adult world and to show an answer for adults. Although Thurber has known the power of the imagination in all of
his sketches in the 1930's, he only now learns how to dramatize
a triumphant vision; one of the stories ends with a marriage festi-
val, the classic way for comedies to end. The Romance provides
Thurber with another form (like the fable) by means of which he
can fulfill the writer's ancient duty of advising man on his true
condition. Behind the guise of a fairy tale he can speak of a world
of ideals and delight his reader in the process. He puts real toads,
as Marianne Moore advises the writer to do, in an imaginary garden.

The Vision

Since Wordsworth wrote his "Preface" to *Lyrical Ballads*, our
writers have looked more at experience than at the heroic ideals
animating civilization. The trivia of experience is the modern plague;
it does not kill with swift sureness or violent pain, as Malory's
plague did, but it does kill with boredom. There is no plague of
trivia in the children's stories. The world is distant, charming, and
so complete that we bask in full pleasure in it. Thurber has all the
delightful paraphernalia of Kings, Royal Astronomers, Dukes,
Jesters, Wizards, Magicians, and Beautiful Ladies. He even has
Morgan le Fay (Thurber turns the name around to make it Nagrom
Yaf), the villainess of Arthurian romances. Clearly the world is
displaced from our trauma. The images are the general images of
distance: the Princess is fair, red-lipped, and full-figured. The
architecture is gothic and labyrinthine. The landscape is formal,
and the language is innocent and naive. Whole scenes are repeated
like responses to ritualistic question. In moments of high excitement, characters break into rhythmic speech. In the last three
books, Thurber closes scenes with couplets as did the Elizabethan
playwrights. The foreground is filled and completed by the rich
fabric of the artist's invention; we stand in presence chambers,
ride through enchanted landscapes, and view complete courts and
villages. All is cool, serene, and formed so that the hero may indeed

act and know a truer essence than we know in our experience.

But at our backs we always hear—the trauma of our times. The echo is neither loud nor insistent, but gentle and suggestive. The King in *Many Moons* turns to a counselor and snarls incongruously, "Don't tell me everything you've done for me since 1907." The giant ravaging the landscape in *The Great Quillow* is named *Hunder*, suggesting *Hun* and *plunder* and reminding us of the World Wars. King Clode in *The White Deer* behaves like a well-meaning executive of a medium-sized corporation in tax trouble. In *The Thirteen Clocks*, a tag line from Gilbert and Sullivan—"a thing of shreds and patches"—identifies the wandering minstrel. The villains in *The Wonderful O* recall Robert Louis Stevenson villains or a Congressional investigating committee. In these stories the present hovers in our subconscious just as the Earl of Warwick, the Father of Courtesy, hovers behind Malory's King Arthur. In Thurber, however, the incongruity has a comic function and encourages us to recognize that the echo of the present is constant, that the subject matter is really our subject matter and not the mere story of jesters and giants. The landscape is, in fact, our landscape of waste and confusion.

Each Eden has a blight. Each story begins with a representation of a wasted landscape. In *Many Moons* the young Princess is sick; unless her father can get her the moon, she will die. *The Great Quillow* has two wastelands: one is potential and physical, represented by a giant's threat to lay waste the village in three weeks; the other wasteland is represented by the minds of the town councilmen who ineffectually scramble to discover a plan of appeasement. *The White Deer* begins with King Clode and two of his sons disconsolately enduring existence; for the third time in the century, they have destroyed all the game in the kingdom. Since they have no task or function (recall George Smith in *Is Sex Necessary?*), life is gone from the kingdom. At the end of *The White Deer,* when Thurber writes his first marriage scene and classic end of comedy, King Clode stands, somewhat unsteadily but triumphantly, and shouts: "Surrounded by these dodderers and dolts, I blow my horn in waste land, so to speak." The wasteland in *The Thirteen Clocks* takes the form of coldness. The Duke is so cold that he wears gloves at all times; he refuses to give the hand of the Princess Saralinda in marriage "since her hand [is] the only warm hand in the castle." When the Princess enters the room, the Duke holds "up the palms of his gloves, as if she were a fire at which to warm his hands." In *The Wonderful O* the land is laid waste by robbery. The villains Black and Littlejack not only remove all of the *o* words from the language including *love, hope,* and *valor,* but they ransack villages, cities and burial sites to find pelf and jewels (not money and gold in tombs). Thus in each of the five books, infertility is the basic fact from which the action begins. The infertility presents the coldness, the inanition, the robbery and plundering so familiar to us. Thurber never insists that this world is our own; as an artist, he presents a vision, and we recognize it.

The reader's attention in the typical romance focuses completely on the struggle between good and evil; the hero faces the paralysis of the wasteland (evil) and finds a way to recreate society. To magnify the tension between the opponents in Thurber's stories, conventional Men of Power try obvious and practical solutions to relieve the infertility. A king turns to his advisers; a town council asks its members to suggest solutions; lawyers are called in. The application of power—intellect, economics, laws—fails and actually increases and threatens the world in the tale. As we recognize the wasteland condition, we further recognize the power which ineffectually tries to bring back life and meaning, for the Men of Power are the equivalents in the world of romance for businessmen, scientists, philosophers, and lawyers. Their inevitable failure sends the land deeper into its infertility and prepares us to rejoice more in the hero's final triumph.

Many Moons, the first of these books published, readily shows Thurber's serious purpose by its presentation of these Men of Power. The King calls three advisers to ask them to get the moon, for his daughter will die unless she can have it. Each adviser responds with a long list of services performed, and from the list we discover that the advisers are archetypes or representatives of the modern dilemma. The Lord High Chamberlain announces pontifically to the King that he has

> . . .got ivory, apes and peacocks, rubies, opals, and emeralds, black orchids, pink elephants and blue poodles, gold bugs, scarabs, and flies in amber, hummingbirds' tongues, angels' feathers, and unicorns' horns, giants, midgets, and mermainds, frank-

incense, ambergris, and myrrh, troubadors, minstrels and dancing women.

The Lord High Chamberlain has, in short, brought all the joys and wealth of the world to the King; in the world of romance, he represents the prodigious success of commerce and distribution in ministering to the King. Thurber's energetic catalogue makes attractive what the businessman has brought. We are allowed no superficial judgment which condemns businessmen, for what the Chamberlain offers is worthy and admirable. Unfortunately the businessman cannot help at the critical moment in the King's rule: he cannot get the moon for the Princess Lenore.

The King next summons his Royal Wizard to get the moon to save the life of the dying Princess. He too has a long list of wonders wrought:

> I have squeezed blood out of turnips for you, and turnips out of blood. I have produced rabbits out of silk hats, and silk hats out of rabbits. I have conjured up flowers, tambourines, and doves. I have brought you divining rods, magic wands, and crystal spheres in which to behold the future. I have compounded philters, unguents, and potions, to cure heartbreak, surfeit, and ringing of the ears. I have made you my own special mixture of wolfbane, nightshade, and eagle's tears, to ward off witches, demons, and things that go bump in the night. I have given you seven league boots, the golden touch, and a cloak of invisibility . . .horns from elfland, sand from the Sandman, and gold from the rainbow.

Again we are dazzled by the adviser's offerings. The catalogue now, however, contains sheer wizardry and marvel. His list stands for the wealth that the technician and the scientist bring to us. But while his list too is convincing and marvelous, the Royal Wizard cannot bring life back into the kingdom by granting the wish of the languishing Princess for the moon. The Wizard's failure is the failure of technical society to ease human need (although it has done much for human want); he has much to offer but little to offer in the present human case.

In despair, the King turns to a third hired assistant, the Royal Mathematician. Again the counsellor repeats a list of marvels, for the Mathematician has

figured out [for the King] the distance between the horns of
a dilemma, night and day, and A and Z. [He has] computed how
far is Up, how long it takes to get to Away, and what becomes
of Gone. [He has] discovered the length of the sea serpent, the
price of the priceless, and the square of the hippopotamus. [He
knows] where you are when you are at Sixes and Sevens, how
much Is you have to have to make Are, and how many birds
you can catch with the salt of the ocean — 187,796,132 if it would
interest you to know.

While superficially similar to the other lists and similar in that
it too is an attractive series of accomplishments performed, the
final listing has a quality of terror, of search into unknowable
unknowns. The question of how much *Is* it takes to make *Are* calls
to our minds the modern physicists and linguistic philosophers
who probe so deeply into our universe. Since the Royal Mathematician, the abstract philosopher of our world of experience,
cannot obtain the moon any more than the other two, the sterility
and threat linger. All is dark within the house, or the palace in
this case, and our desire for a moment of light is intensified. The
stage is set for the entrance of the hero, the man of imagination.

The other four books show the same unsuccessful effort to
vitalize a wasted land. In *The Great Quillow* the businessmen on
the town council offer ludicrous but common sense plans to drive
off the Giant Hunder. The Tailor suggests putting needles in the
suit the Giant has ordered; the Cobbler wants to put nails in his
new boots. These respected men — who offer important services
to their community in their shoes, clothes and food — cannot meet
the special demands of the new threat. In *The White Deer* a bumbling and ineffectual Palace Wizard, a Royal Recorder, a Royal
Physician, and a Royal Astronomer (who looks at the sky through
a pink-tinted telescope) all fail. In *The Thirteen Clocks* "taverners,
travelers, taletellers, tosspots, troublemakers and townspeople"
offer barroom witticism to counter the fearful threat. In *The Wonderful O* the island lawyer, a man who should aid the community
defense against the robbers and brigands, actually joins forces
with the invading host, Quisling-like, and helps to harry the land.
The island-dwellers themselves are so overwhelmed by the threat
of Black and Littlejack that they wait for their own extinction like

patient sheep (or the Jews in Europe) and watch their green and pleasant isle suffer greater and greater depredation. Thus in the displaced world of romance Thurber makes a significant comment about our civilization. Without the slightest sense of ridicule and without coruscating irony (without becoming his enemy and using the enemy tactics), Thurber's world of romance recreates powerful agents in our society and shows that they are pitifully unable to serve in crises that go beyond ordinary mundane problems. The lawyers and businessmen in the world of romance are perfectly capable of solving questions of law and business, while the scientists are able to explain the phenomenal world, but all of them are incapable of solving problems of human meaning. And each failure of these important men — and they must be highly respected men or else the hero's final victory is hollow or anti-climactic — prepares us for the hero's triumph.

To communicate the idea of infertility and of the ineffectuality of the Men of Power, all of the books (except for *Many Moons*) employ the death of time as a metaphor. Not only is the land wasted, but because ordinary men cannot do anything to replenish life, time itself strangely disappears. Thurber makes the connection between time and events wittily in *The Great Quillow*: the hero, we are told, looks like a dandelion clock (*clock* is the gardener's term for the seeds on a dandelion head). The epithet both communicates the fertility of the toymaker's mind and connects him with the time ritual in the story. We are told that Quillow's most treasured gift to his community before the giant arrived was his design of "the twelve scarlet men who emerged from the dial of the town clock on the stroke of every hour." The Giant Hunder, in contrast, "could wrench a clock from its steeple as easily as a child might remove a peanut from its shell." The story comes to its triumphant end with a lovely sentence recounting the return of time: "There the giant was seen no more, and the troubled waters quieted as the sea resumed its inscrutable cycle of tides under the sun and moon." In *The White Deer* the sun goes out (and thus time stops) when King Clode and his sons go hunting for the deer at the beginning of the book. We are told that one of the good wizards "played with time" in order to effect the end of the story. The villain-Duke in *The Thirteen Clocks* roundly declares his enmity to time:

> . . .I slew [time]. . .and wiped my bloody sword upon its beard
> . . . .If there were light, I'd show you on my sleeves the old brown
> stains of seconds, where they bled and died. I slew time in these
> gloomy halls, and wiped my bloody blade—

The final sentence in the speech trails off, for even the Duke is
outside of time. In *The Wonderful O*, Black and Littlejack destroy
time as their first act on the island, and at the end of the book
their defeat is marked by the ringing of a bell which signals the
return of time. Arrested time not only represents the death that
ramps through these kingdoms, but it represents, more necessarily, the loss of contact with human experience that marks Thurber's villains. *Now* is pulsating and alive, but *Then* is cold, con-
trollable, and abstract. The ineffectual solutions offered by the
businessmen, the lawyers, the philosophers, and scientists cannot
penetrate from the abstract world of *Then* to enter the human
world of *Now* where the crisis of each story takes place and where
time exists. The simple, but arresting, device distinguishes between knowledge or intellect (the abstract and cold) and intelligence or imagination (creative, warm, and effective). Intellect
functions in the material world; intelligence moves the world of
human meaning.

With the land at waste, with the counselors and wizards impotent, and with the clocks stopped, the world of Thurber's five
small books is ready for the true hero who will bring life and time
back into existence. Each hero is a poet, a maker. He has the power
to penetrate through the phenomena of experience to grasp human
meaning. His power of creation is quite visible. The King in *Many
Moons* summons his Royal Jester: the King needs him only to sing
a sad song to ease despair, but providentially the Jester twice
finds a way to act and bring the dying princess to life. Quillow,
the toymaker, constructs "hearts of gold for the girls of the town
and hearts of oak for the boys." The third son of King Clode softly
strums a lute and composes verses. The Prince in *The Thirteen
Clocks* is a wandering minstrel. *The Wonderful O* has a poet as
its hero. Designating them as poets and makers, however, is not
all that Thurber does to dramatize the idea of the creative intelligence.

In every book, the hero begins at a lowly station and is treated
with contempt. He is an alien, an outsider, whom no one wants.

As Malory's Gareth is a bow ready to release its arrow, so the sad treatment of Thurber's heroes sets them on edge to spring at the critical moment. The King in *Many Moons,* for example, looks upon the Jester as a mere device, an agent to take his mind off the coming death of his child. The town council considers Quillow's work as a toymaker "a rather pretty waste of time." His name suggests that he is a hollow reed or quill which the Council blows around for amusement, winding him up as if he were a toy and refusing to admit him to the council. He is present at their meetings only to provide frivolous amusement. Prince Jorn is more fully a male Cinderella. He is the third son who does not like to hunt as his father and brothers do; he speaks truth when pleasant lies would be more convenient. His father contemptuously bets that his two older brothers will easily accomplish the perilous task set for them. The Minstrel Prince in *The Thirteen Clocks* is jovially mocked in the title Prince of Rags. When the *o* is taken from the poet in *The Wonderful O,* he becomes equal to his dog, for then they are both merely pets. The important men in each society treat the poet-heroes contemptuously.

Lowly as each hero is, he has the power to discover the categories of human meaning. Hs alone acts to bring life and time back into the wasteland, and since he acts after the conventional men of power have failed, his triumph indeed dazzles the reader. Thus the Jester in *Many Moons,* noting that the Chamberlain, Wizard, and Mathematician all describe the moon differently, asks the Princess what the moon is and how large it is. The Princess says that it is no larger than her thumbnail; it is no higher than the tree outside her window; and it is made of gold. The Jester promises to climb the tree that very evening and bring it to her; in fact, he goes to the Goldsmith and has him make a golden moon according to the Jester's instructions.

> The Court Jester took the moon to the Princess Lenore, and she was overjoyed. The next day she was well again and could get up and go out in the gardens to play.

The Jester's pattern of creative intelligence saves each wasteland. Quillow stages a campaign of psychological warfare and convinces the Giant that he has some frightful disease which can only be cured by plunging himself into the sea. Although King Clode and his two eldest sons see "the false flux of fact and form" in their pursuit of the White Deer, Prince Jorn penetrates to what is true in the character of the deer magically transformed into a Princess who has "a memory of fields and meadows, and a memory of nothing more." The hero of *The Thirteen Clocks* needs the full time help of a supernatural agent called the Golux; the Golux, however, clearly represents the power of the imagination. *The Wonderful O* is the most explicit of the five stories; Andreus, the poet, invokes the power of men in fairy tale and legend to defeat Black and Littlejack. In every case, the creative imagination, the poet's power, discovers the secret of fertility to bring life and time back into the dead kingdom.

Thus Thurber dramatizes that high idea of the imagination which enables the poet to "build that dome in air," as Coleridge said, to give life its rich significance and meaning. Meaning, the stories say, does not exist in the world of phenomena; meaning is imposed by the mind, and the mind of the poet—the maker— discovers the meaning for the human heart. Thurber refines and dramatizes the quality of creative intelligence in these books just as Malory's heroes dramatize *courtoisie* and *gentilesse.* Thurber's quality is defined by the foils that he sets beside his heroes so that in contrast to the foil, the true imagination of the hero forces itself into the reader's mind. In *The White Deer* two separate kinds of wizards affect the action: the King's ineffectual palace wizards and the very successful wood wizards who are allied to Prince Jorn, the hero. The palace wizards have been trained in the abstract laws of their science; the wood wizards have acquired a further measure of understanding which we would call the genius of the creative imagination. King Clode diagnoses the failure of the palace wizards:

> Average wood wizards know more in one day than this buffoon [his own palace wizard] learns in ten years, spite of the fact he attended one of the most expensive schools for sorcerers in the world. Bah! can't teach a man to ride a horse or cast a spell. Comes naturally or it doesn't come at all.

The wood wizards, in contrast, have the instinctive sense of identification and creation; this sense comes as the leaves of the tree. Prince Jorn shares this ability, for when he sees the White Deer

who is transformed into a Princess, he is not impelled by any irritable reaching after fact or reason as are the palace wizards. He
simply loves her. The same naturalness and directness enables
the Princess Saralinda to start the thirteen clocks; although "Tinkers
and tinkerers and a few wizards who happened by tried to start
the clocks with tools or magic words, or by shaking them and
cursing," the Princess starts them by *not* touching them. We might
compare the quality of the wood wizards and Thurber's heroes
with *instinct* in animals, but instinct suggests a mindless quality.
It is mindless if we mean by mind the operation of inductive and
deductive logic. The quality goes beyond logic to that intuitive,
non-discursive grasp of categories of meaning.

If I suggest that these stories should be read as allegories,
I have created a wrong impression. They are stories which follow
a pattern of meaning: the human imagination is alone capable of
comprehending and solving the human situation. The vision may
not satisfy all: T. S. Eliot's Anglo-Catholic tradition, absurdists
facing absurdity, social causes like Marxism, Liberalism, or Con-
servatism offer quite different ways of seeing the human experience. The important thing about Thurber is that he can show us
the power of the artist and the power of the practical man of affairs without denigrating practical men or traditionalists or Marxists. Inside his faith in the creative imagination, his art finds a
way to allow his men and women to act. And thus once more he
creates, by his vision, a dome or a mountain from which to view
the plain of ordinary experience. An artist can do little more.

The Method

As we have seen in the fables, Thurber's stories for children
provide that essential architecture upon which to display his artistry. My illustrations have already demonstrated the marvelous
vitality and energy of his language. Withdrawn from their context,
his devices and techniques look deliberate. One illustration from
the beginning of *The White Deer* may be extracted because the
paragraph is not so deeply embedded in the book's total theme.
The Royal Recorder is reading all the names of Kings in hopes
that the Princess (the former White Deer) might remember her
father's name. He stops his list because the ineffectual Palace

Wizard has dropped a ball he was juggling and made the Princess jump in surprise. Thinking that he might have found the girl's father and thus her history, the Recorder comments on the particular king mentioned when she jumped. Thurber prints the speech, of course, as prose, but the perceptive reader senses a rhythm in the speech that is close to blank verse. For the sake of analysis, I copy it as if it were verse.

> "King Puggy," he said disapprovingly,
> "Is the most disreputable king in the Whole Registry of Kings:
> He lives in a ruined castle on a hill
> With his seven madcap daughters.
> The Old King's wife died of a fit of shrieks
> When all the Princesses were very young. Now
> Puggy and his seven maids live all alone,
> Wreaking every kind of hob and havoc on their hill:
> Rolling boulders down on passersby,
> Turning rivers from their normal course,
> Stealing gems and silks from caravans
> So they can dress in gaudy masquerade
> And play their wild and eerie games by jack-o'-lantern light."
> The Royal Recorder raised his hands and shook his head.
> "Every night is Halloween on Puggy's Hill."

Obviously Thurber has not written the speech in iambic pentameter verse, but the speech is close enough to verse so that seeing it as verse one can better describe his handling. It starts in ordinary speech rhythm, but then one begins to feel the rhythm of iambs — unaccented syllable followed by an accented syllable. "He lives in a ruined castle on a hill" is not perfect iambic pentameter line, but its rhythm is more insistent than speech. As the Recorder gets caught in his story, the accent shifts from iambs to trochees — *i.e.,* the accent now falls on the first syllable:

> Rolling boulders down on passersby,
> Turning rivers from their normal course,
> Stealing gems and silks from caravans.

In the Wizard's comment on the scene, the accent shifts again and we sense the unaccented syllable coming first.

> So they can dress in gaudy masquerade
> And play their wild and eerie games by jack-o'-lantern light.

When the speech ends, and Thurber turns to describe an action performed by the recorder, the language returns to the original speech rhythm of its beginning: "The Royal Recorder raised his hands and shook his head." The final words about Puggy, "Every night is Halloween on Puggy's Hill," again give the first syllable of the metrical foot a strong accent. Such handling is very witty, very enjoyable, and, in its own way, beautiful. Although some of his late realistic stories (realistic only in contrast to these stories) also use subtle speech rhythms, Thurber cannot exploit the language so successfully in them.

At another point in *The White Deer* the language becomes lyrical and, at the same time, reverses our language expectations so that we are delighted with a new vision. Thag, one of the older sons, enters a wood on his quest for the treasure that will win the Princess. Although the wood is a strange and frightening place, the world of romance places it far enough away from normal experience so that it entertains without confronting us with direct and frightening fact. Thag meets a strange creature in the "crouch" of a tree. At one point in the jabberwocky, the following interchange takes place:

> High up in a tree, a chock climbed slowly.
> "I wonder what type it is?" said Thag.
> "It's sick thirsty, " said the man, "or half past hate or a quarter to fight. I'm in no moon for questions.
> "You're in no *mood*," said Thag.
> "First he accosts me, then he tells me what I'm not in," said the man. "I crutch in the crouch of this tree to avoid troublemakers like you, riding on their nagamuffins."

Thag cannot reduce anything to meaning, and the more that he tries, the deeper he becomes entangled. The mad combat ends (one thinks of *Alice in Wonderland*) when Thag's adversary shouts, "A plague on both your horses!" and the young knight goes riding toward the shining Valley of Euphoria. To the practical-minded Thag, the whole interchange is utter nonsense, but the reader is teased by a reality behind the confusing words.

When Prince Jorn finds himself in a similar situation, he penetrates behind the false flux of fact and form. Jorn defeats a fierce Black Knight who guards the orchard where Jorn has found the

thousand rubies. When the Knight falls, Jorn discovers that he
has the head and face of a man of seventy.

> "I would not have fought so venerable a knight had I known,"
> said Jorn.
> "You fought the fearful thing I seemed to be, and that's the
> test and proof of valor, that's the proof and test. When all is dark
> within the house, who knows the monster from the mouse?"

Thag, in contrast, has not fought. To every confusion, he answers
with his own thick tongue in a futile attempt to impose a logical
meaning on the interchange. Jorn, using his human power, penetrates the chink in the Black Knight's armor and learns the reality:
"You fought the fearful thing I seemed to be." The language of
The White Deer by its method supports the meaning of the story.
The language shows that meaning is found in the mind and not in
objects themselves. As in the example of the Royal Recorder telling
the story of King Puggy, the exploitation of language delights the
reader in its artistry.

In *The Thirteen Clocks* the language drives us to the deeper
and richer meaning that these books demand. The Golux (the aide
who calls himself a Mere Device) and the hero draw near the house
of Hagga, a woman who once wept jewels. Alliteration and asso-
nance communicate the maze where the hero and the Golux find
themselves:

> The brambles and the thorns grew thick and thicker in a
> ticking thicket of bickering crickets. Farther along and stronger,
> bonged the gongs of a throng of frogs, green and vivid on their
> lily pads. From the sky came the crying of flies, and the pilgrims
> leaped over a bleating sheep creeping knee-deep in a sleepy stream,
> in which swift and slippery snakes slid and slithered silkily,
> whispering sinful secrets.

As always in these books, the prose recreates the experience so
that its parts add up to a greater whole than logic tells us is there.

The five books are also rich in texture because of their allusions, inventiveness, and traditional motifs. I have been delighted
to discover the number three used as a pattern in *The Great Quillow*. Three is a magic number of romance, and nearly everything
in the book happens in a three-part rhythm: there are three hundred people in the village; the giant must have three sheep to eat

every day; his depredations will plunder the village in three weeks; the third symptom of the Giant's malady drives him to the ocean and his death. In *The White Deer* the hero is the third son and his third quest is successful. The books contain ambiguities to keep critics busy for years to discover the large and rich meaning of each. These pleasures bring the reader back to the books again and again.

I do not suggest, of course, that Thurber self-consciously loaded his books with language and rhetorical devices for the sake of giving them their rich texture. In his effort to give the quest motif of each book its fullest realization, however, he naturally and simply (like the characters in the books themselves) turns to every conscious and subconscious device to support his basic theme of the imaginative intelligence. As the Princess Saralinda in *The Thirteen Clocks* started the clocks by *not* touching them, so we should read these books by letting their dramatic impact hit us directly. My point is that they communicate to us in many more ways than we consciously realize.

The Criticism of Life

I apologize to Thurber's shade for reducing his art to a formula, for making him a twentieth-century comic Coleridge with a strong sense of design. He has, however, both the intelligence and design or, in other words, both form and content.

He says, in a statement that seems to contradict his practice in these books, "I am blessed or cursed, whichever it may be, by an inherited gift of taste that leans toward real girls on trains, crazy or not, and away from mixies and pixies and nymphs." If he prefers real girls, one may well ask, why then does he choose to write five books about kings, jesters, and princesses? The apparent contradiction is explained by the fact that the five books concern real ideals. They have about them a distinct sense of fact, for royal wizards do exist in our society. We do not find royal wizards in our commuting trains, but we do find everywhere their ideals of abstract, cold order. Fortunately we also have in Thurber himself a jester who is quite real and not a mixie, a pixie, or a nymph.

In the five books which I call Romances Thurber sustained his most creative flight. Except in these books (and possibly in *The Male Animal*) Thurber always follows the injunction to the comic writer that he be short and swift. Even the shortest of these stories, *Many Moons,* is several times the length of his usual sketch, and *The White Deer* and *The Wonderful O* come near to the length of a short novel. I am not going to argue in favor of these books because of their length, but I can notice that his art has a deeper meaning here because we sense an interplay between a larger pattern of surface perception—the quest-motif of romance—and the pressures of depth-perception which makes us see that he writes about a power that exists in our civilization, the power that gives us ivory, apes, and peacocks but cannot give us the moon or free us from plundering giants, idiot rulers, and robbers. In the larger space of these books, he has room to define those qualities of the Jester which can bring life back into our wasted land suffering its surfeit of ivory and peacocks.

I see one more convincing reason Thurber writes five books for children that make their reader see relationships between them and the work of a romancer like Sir Thomas Malory. In spite of the many similarities, one great difference is apparent: Malory wrote for a world without comforts, a world that had to dream about a condition in which one would have the leisure to think of high ideals. We live in a world that each day belies the most extravagant of romances, for physical discomfort has nearly disappeared. We may have spiritual trauma, but we are surrounded by more servants than King Clode had in his entire retinue. Our servants are mechanical gadgets that may fail like living servants, but they relieve us of the burden of ordinary repetitive labor and *we* live the life of romance. Four-fifths of us have riches beyond King Arthur and his Table to imagine; even those technically classed as poverty-stricken drive automobiles and own television sets. The fulness of romance is no longer an imagined Golden Clime, but it is an American fact, and the American fact is rapidly becoming the world's pain. Instead of laboring to obtain existence, we live in affluence; what now is a man to do? In the past men sublimated their desires (Freud spoke of infant sexuality) to a reality principle (again Freud's term), but now the pleasures of romance are available twenty-four hours a day. I have heard a scientist say that the time is nearly in our sight when man will not *have* to die but will live like King Clode. We will be, then, outside of time just as the villains in these stories are outside of time. All is dark, however, within our house unless the Poet or Jester can tell us which is the monster and which the mouse. With ivory, apes, and peacocks at our call, we desperately need the man who can give us light and make our time run. Thurber's stories, therefore, justify the artist and make the Brave New World's need of him apparent. Without the artist, the world does not look brave at all.

Thurber, then, has not just chosen an available form, but he has chosen the one form that communicates the reality of our experience. He writes about a world in which the dream of pleasure is the commonplace. He writes about a real world where time is stopped. Now more than ever before the imaginative intelligence is needed to give value and significance to our real gardens. What begins by arousing our laughter—the comic incongruity between an imagined world and fact—turns out to be more than a comic device. It is a means of commenting on and understanding our strange and bizarre experience.

VIII

The Unsound
and the Fuzzy

This survey now comes to the final period of Thurber's work, that period when his admirers scanned the Master's publications to see whether he was continuing to develop or whether age was laying its inevitable pall. Of the six books at the end the master's touch is clearest in *The Thurber Album* (1952) and *The Years With Ross* (1959); the touch also still animates many pieces in the four collections: *Thurber Country* (1953), *Alarms and Diversions* (1957), *Lanterns and Lances* (1961) and the posthumous *Credos and Curios* (1962). In the *Album* and *Ross*, to use catch titles, Thurber achieves a more human comedy than before, a comedy that laughs with the hero in his triumph. Less successful pieces in the collections bluntly condemn or praise what *Ross* and *Album* give by vision. In both *Album* and *Ross,* Thurber reminisces about a world as remote as the far world in the stories for children where ideals and ideas exist in full flower. The *Album* explores late nineteenth-century and early twentieth-century America when the human self could "be" without the frustrations and limitations of our sad and lonely time. Harold Ross, with all his contraditions, is a product of nineteenth-century America triumphing over the unsound and fuzzy world of his writers, his competitors, and the time itself. In these books a master creates Ross and the men and women in the *Album* as human beings acting themselves in a comic vision.

The men and women in *Ross* and *Album* walk across a catastrophic stage. In these books Ross, Jacob Fisher, Aunt Margery Albright, Mary Agnes Thurber and others endure and prevail. They triumph at the expense of a civilization which can no longer produce such men and women. At one moment in the *Album*, his mask drops and we see Thurber's aim clearly:

> Group civilization, they tell me, has come to the corner of Parsons Avenue and Bryden Road, where my grandfather built his house in the year 1884, well beyond stone's throw of his nearest neighbor, and I suppose the individual has taken on the gray color of the mass. But there were individuals about during the first decade of the century, each possessed of his own bright and separate values.

Thurber's syntax, usually so pellucid and logical, obscures his meaning. The sentence says that group civilization has come and caused the individual to take on "the gray color of the mass," but the long interruption about his grandfather's house obtrudes between the awareness and the conclusion. Like the bright and separate values, the house stands out above the disappointing thought. The particular essay in which Thurber's mask drops presents men low in the scale of society; nevertheless they exist as human beings who could then—but not now—achieve their comic triumph. By implication we sense our group civilization which makes odd-jobs men, stablemen, and blind asylum workers mere cogs in a vast machine. In the first decades of the century these men could act; now they stare stupidly at television sets. The catastrophic stage is also apparent in *Ross*, for the drama is enacted in the 1930's and 1940's when the mist or gray color nearly engulfs all.

In *Ross* and *Album* creative minds heal and bring meaning in spite of the approaching grayness. Mrs. Thurber naturally endowed her world, and *Ross* was born to create the *New Yorker*. Stablemen and odd-jobs men make the world bright and interesting. These men and women illustrate the creative intelligence and the patience and accuracy that imagination depends on; they have a natural quality of distinction and, most obviously, a ringing vitality. If all men have nerves, these have extra nerves with a higher degree of sensitivity. They not only perceive the world around them, they also create the world in which they live. Their liveness triumphs over the unsoundness and fuzziness of their world and thus provides the comic catharsis. When we experience the sense of joy in Mrs. Thurber or Ross, we are also aware of a civilization that seemingly has no need for their vitality, intelligence, or accuracy. Thurber's view of mid-twentieth-century civilization approaches the despair of Juvenal or the despair of the author of Ecclesiastes, for our society destroys the very quality and talent which give it meaning and value.

The Thurber Album makes palpable and exact those social qualities which Thurber praises and those social qualities which he condemns. In *Thurber Country, Lanterns and Lances, Alarms and Diversions*, and *Credos and Curios* the self struggles, not always successfully, to realize its own bright and separate values. In *The Years with Ross* a creative mind faces a destructive society to wrest value from it. Ross is, I believe, the perfect Thurber hero, demonstrating finally and completely Thurber's vision as a comic writer.

Laughter With

Although Thurber's books in the 1930's and 1940's all have a consistent point of view, *The Thurber Album* differs from them because its laughter is all a celebration. The book laughs with the humanity of its characters, and it thus celebrates their power of life and their joy and gaiety.

Thurber told a *Paris Review* interviewer shortly after he finished the book, "I wanted to write the story of some solid American characters, more or less as an example of how Americans started out and what they should go back to—to sanity and soundness and away from this jumpiness." The solid Americans are his grandparents, his relatives, friends, the newspapermen he knew in Columbus, and three of his teachers at Ohio State University. If it be a standard comic work, *Album* is written backward, for it starts with its heroes and ends with quasi-heroes who evoke more pity than joy. The book ends in the wasteland where the books for children begin. It starts in sanity and soundness and ends in jumpiness; it juxtaposes the solid past against lesser men of the near past to dramatize a loss of vitality in the American character.

Thurber's choice of men and women for his album further demonstrates his effort to achieve a coherent structure. Although he speaks often of his infallible memory, Thurber writes of two men whom he could have only known casually. The chapter on Bob Ryder, editor and paragrapher of the *Ohio State Journal*, gives us a man whom Thurber met once when Thurber was a third-year student in high school. Thurber spent no more than three days in the fall of 1916 with Mr. Ziegfeld of "Snapshot of Mr. Ziegfeld." From family memory and a few scraps of printed evidence he creates two ancestors whom he could not have known. These men all fit the book's pattern of progression from a rich and vital past to a sterile and debilitating present.

Comparing the *Album* with *My Life and Hard Times*, a book also heavily freighted with relatives and friends in Columbus, proves that Thurber had a clear intention in mind when he returned to his past. The early book concentrates on comic madness, but the second book looks back to define what qualities made his grandfather and his mother the sound, interesting, and exciting people they were. Grandfather in *My Life* has the same adventure with an electric runabout that Grandfather William Fisher has in the *Album*. Both men are eccentric enough for comedy, but the earlier grandfather is a conventional comic stereotype; the second grandfather is a man trapped by a machine. The reader remembers the antic behavior of Grandpa in *My Life*, but he remembers the humanity of Grandfather Fisher. In both versions the grandfather approaches the vehicle as if it were a wild colt, but in the first version the machine totally defeats him. Grandfather Fisher, however, learned well enough to operate it; he simply could not master the finer requirements of backing. In both cases the grandparent drives the car into a ditch, but the purpose of the story differs. The first exploits Grandpa's anger. In the second version, Grandfather Fisher accepts his defeat. In the *Album* the story ends:

> It took a garage man [against two workmen and a farmhand in *My Life*] an hour to get us loose and on the road again. Grandpa paid him and said, in his bluffest manner, "Drop in at the store and I'll give you a watermelon." He was forever trying to cover up embarrassing situations by offering people watermelons.

The scene recalls the food offering to propitiate the gods in Greek comedy; Grandfather Fisher does not get angry nor shout imprecations but offers a watermelon on the altar of humanity and the auto mechanic. Because he failed to master the runabout, "he kept his horse and surrey years after his friends had turned to the auto- mobile." We see no picture of Grandfather Fisher getting into comic difficulties with his surrey in Columbus traffic; Thurber does not exploit an obvious comic possibility. The first book denies the human being for the sake of laughter, but the second book upholds Grandfather Fisher and discovers its laughter in his humanity. The first book treats of events; the second treats people. *My Life* may be, as Thurber said to the *Paris Review,* "a funnier book," but I doubt if it is necessarily, as Thurber went on to say, "a better book." If judgment is based on the amount of laughter, one may laugh aloud more often reading *My Life and Hard Times* than *The Thurber Album,* but the satisfaction of human perception is greater in *The Thurber Album.*

The *Album* praises Grandfather Fisher's humanity for his ability to accept the world in which he lives. We laugh at him when he carries a rose in his mouth like a cigar; we laugh at his diffi- culties with the runabout; we laugh at his propensity to have his picture taken on any occasion. Our laughter, much muted in com- parison to the laughter at Grandpa in *My Life and Hard Times,* serves the purpose of pointing to a quality that Grandfather Fisher had, the quality of self-discipline. In sheer physical vitality, Grandfather Fisher is a comedown from his own father, a man who threw an opponent in a fistfight twenty-five feet, picked up a horse, and tore a railroad box car to pieces because of an injustice. If Grandfather Fisher is not the physical specimen his father was, he does have his own heroism. He establishes a successful busi- ness, and he pays back $50,000 that friends had invested in a gold mining venture that he had unwisely sponsored. His favorite words to his grandchildren when they face adversity are "Show your Fisher." Grandfather Fisher and all the solid Americans in the early part of the book have this sense of self-direction, this instinct to act upon the world to give it purpose.

Two women easily dominate the book: Aunt Margery Albright and Mary Agnes Thurber. Thurber's own inventive genius might well have come from his mother, for she was a woman able to transform almost any material into a comic invention. The two women are much like the jesters, toymakers, and poets in the books for children. Aunt Margery is also, like them, an outcast from society, and like them she has marvelous powers: she grows flowers, heals the sick, and makes her house a place of enchantment. She is, Thurber writes, a woman "fit, it seemed to me, to be the mother of King Arthur." Although she has an injured leg that would incarcerate a modern woman for the rest of her life, Aunt Margery's sense of self-discipline and even patience with her infirmity keep her moving and acting. A large part of Thurber's vision of the woman is given to her collection of herbs and her recipes for home remedies. Although her remedies seem quaint and possibly futile (she cures Thurber's father with cold coffee), she touches life and experience more fully than later men and women. She lives deliberately. She knows "dozens of roots and leaves and barks, good for everything from ache to agony and from pukin' spells to a knotted gut." She knows her world and, however unsatisfactory it may seem to us, converts her experience into understanding.

Another quality of the solid American character is the care and accuracy employed to understand the world. Not one of the men and women in the *Album* takes the world's false flux for granted. Mr. Ziegfeld, for example, is a Democratic registrar with whom Thurber works during the elections of 1916. Someone has written on the walls of their portable polling place, "*A bas le professeur.*" Mr. Ziegfeld cannot forget the sign; he ponders who might have written such a sign in the working class neighborhood the polling booth served and what he might have meant by it. Mr. Ziegfeld was

> a born controversialist, a man in love with the debatable aspects of life. He was an expert carpenter and all-around craftsman, who could fix anything that was broken in a house, from cellar to attic. He liked to take apart contraptions and ideas, to see what made them tick and to find out if they were soundly put together and made of good materials. He knew that the constructions and conclusions of men had a satisfying shape, and gave out a satisfying sound, only if they were right.

Others in the early part of the book show this same care and accuracy. Sam Bell, Jacob Fisher, Charles Thurber (his father), and Mary Agnes Thurber have a driving urge to reduce chaos to order and significance. Like Mr. Ziegfeld, they all might have had a sign on their house reading, "Points Argued, Principles Stated, Opinions Changed," for they all grasped at human experience to impose their own minds and energies on it.

Further, the *Album* defends the distinction and dignity of the individual in its heroes. The words sound undemocratic in the group civilization, and Thurber has to take some pains to show that his natural aristocrats themselves achieve their own excellence. Aunt Margery deserved the title of mother of Arthur. Another is Jacob Fisher, Thurber's great-grandfather, a man who

> fought men who were hard on their womenfolks or were cruel
> to dumb animals, but mostly he fought to back up his political
> beliefs or to defend the divine inspiration of Scripture: "There
> is too goddam much blasphemin' goes on," he used to say.

He is a natural aristocrat with the courage to "sit down at table with a Negro" even though this action affronts his Presbyterian neighbors. Like a true hero, he has the strength to pick up a horse "in his arms and [move] it eight or ten feet away" before he starts a fight. He owned ten thousand acres of land, and he fought for the right to travel the toll road without paying the expected fee, a bargain that he had made with the toll company but a bargain that the company's gate keepers did not honor until Jacob Fisher made them honor it. By their own efforts the solid Americans elevate themselves to distinction and dignity.

In the early part of *The Thurber Album* especially, the men and women have the energy to challenge fortune and deny it whatever it asks. Their energy is demonstrated, if by nothing else, by their longevity. Judge Stacy Taylor, a Thurber ancestor, ramped through two states, four or five counties, three wives, and innumerable progeny. He died at the age of eighty-seven. Another relative, Aunt Mary Van York, chewed tobacco until her ninety-third year. William F. Fisher, Thurber's grandfather, did not live as long as his father, the famous Jacob Fisher who died at seventy-seven, but he lived resoundingly. He announced himself in restaurants and hotels as "William F. Fisher of Columbus, Ohio," and he expected lesser men to be impressed. Aunt Margery Albright caught the secret vitality and both she and her daughter lived to be eighty-eight. Not only did they live so long but they lived well. Thurber proposes as an epitaph for his mother a statement made by a friend shortly after her death three weeks short of ninety: "You know...even

if Mame had been the first to go, she would have outlived us all."
As Thurber presents his men and women in his album, they all
overflow with energy and vitality, the gusto for life that the comic
writer requires of his heroes.

In contrast, the men in the final six sketches—the three English
professors and the three newspapermen—lack vitality. Most of
them die younger, or if they manage to preserve life into their
sixth decade, they spend their final years in fruitless activity.
When they do succeed, something equivocable marks their success.
Joseph Taylor, the first of the teachers, publishes a thin book of
Victorian verse, a slight book on composition, and writes long
essays (unpublished) on Henry James and the Tristram and Isolde
legend. Billy Graves, the second teacher, is vulgarized in a popular
magazine biographical sketch, writes a defense of college fraterni-
ties, and ends his life writing rabid editorials in a student newspaper praising Lindbergh and the Nazis. Dean Denney, the strongest
of the lot, has his moments of triumph, but Thurber pointedly ends
his sketch with an illustration showing that the cause Denney
fought for, the cause of academic freedom, is once more receiving
its periodic set-back on the Ohio State campus. Thurber writes of
the man who had once been President of the American Association
of University Professors, that

> Ohio State, trapped somewhere between Armageddon and
> Waterloo, needed him and his strategy of reason and his tactics
> of friendliness, and all the armament of his intellect and his
> humor. But he wasn't there, and there was nobody to take his
> place.

The essay ends on a dying fall: "I like to think that his incomparable
length and shadow have not been completely lost in the towering
and umbrageous wilderness of modern Gigantic Ohio State." The
failure of the Dean's cause remains in our memory.

The newspapermen at the end of the book also fail at their
greatest chance and furthermore they die earlier. Gus Kuehner, the
working newsman who had learned his trade and craft as a police
reporter, resigned at the moment of his achievement. In a final
chapter of the *Album* Thurber tries again to explain what happened to Kuehner. "In trying to slip quietly past the explanation of
his tragic decline," Thurber writes, "I succeeded only in leaving it

provocatively vague." Kuehner's life, a Thurber correspondent suggests, lost its meaning and sense; no jester, toymaker, or wandering minstrel prevented him from becoming a "forlorn and maladjusted managing editor." When he was at the city desk with intimate contact with reporters, his life had meaning, but when he became managing editor, he travelled untrodden ways. With no guide to action, he resigned. Rather than the comic victory and vitality of the men and women early in the book, the reader sees the gray mass seizing and destroying its victim.

The Thurber Album begins in high delight with the spectacle of vigor, vitality, intelligence, courage, and distinction in its nineteenth-century men and women. The book does not change key, for even in the early parts we sense a point of view from another country where life is less a joy; in the final six sketches we watch men ground down by their society. Granted the three English professors and the three newspapermen attempted larger efforts than Jacob Fisher or Aunt Margery Albright. Their influence spread farther than Mary Agnes Thurber's influence or Uncle Jake Matheny's, but the teachers and newsmen all suffer impotence that makes their larger field of action seem ultimately smaller. Kuehner, after his resignation from the newspaper, ended his life working on the swing shift in a warplant. Billy Ireland, dead at fifty-five, has listed among his accomplishments that "He led the campaign to put the quail on the songbird list in Ohio." Ireland (he was cartoonist for the *Dispatch*, Gus Kuehner's paper) is an ineffectual angel. Ryder also—and again in spite of his charm, talent, and intelligence—failed. Thurber quotes a letter Ryder wrote after he retired from the *Ohio State Journal* at the age of fifty-five: "I'd much rather live this way than not live at all." Compare Ryder's response to that of Aunt Margery when her daughter Belle receives a prognosis similar to that which took Ryder from his job and sent him to live in California:

> When Mrs. Albright heard the news, she pushed herself out of her rocking chair and stormed about the room, damning the doctors with such violence that her right knee turned in on her like a flamingo's and she had to be helped back to her chair. Belle recovered from whatever it was that was wrong, and when she died, also at the age of eighty-eight [like her mother], she

had outlived by more than fifteen years the last of the two doctors who had condemned her to death.

Ryder did not storm; he accepted. Why should he storm when he saw all around him an unsoundness and grayness in which life is a pallid and routine thing? In the same letter in which he accepts his lessened life, he writes, "There are almost no honest, independent, courageous newspapers left now. The chainstore variety is rapidly attaining complete domination of the field! No wonder we elect Hoovers and do other unwise things." Ryder's bright and separate values cannot meet the demands of a catastrophic society.

All the teachers and the newspapermen are noble and admirable men defeated by giganticism, by the lack of care for distinction and accuracy, by stupidity and laziness. The *Album* does not lash at these men or at the force that destroys them. It does not argue; it gives the reader a vision. When we compare the journalists and teachers to Mr. Ziegfeld or Aunt Margery Albright, then we know that the voice of the turtle is gone from the land. The early sketches in the book are elegies; the sketches at the end are obituaries. The book's design shows that the wasteland is upon us.

Like the books for children, *The Thurber Album* has faith in the nineteenth-century idea that the individual mind, if it is in contact with the real things of its world, can order those things into a pattern of meaning and value. Thurber treats ministers and politicians respectfully, but his admiration is for the men that Aunt Margery liked: "she liked what she called a man of groin, who could carry his proper share of the daily burden and knew how to tell a sow from a sawbuck." Thurber's comedy in this book is more interested in showing men than it is in provoking laughter; but these men give us a deep and satisfying laughter of the human comedy. Although *My Life and Hard Times* may be a funnier book, *The Thurber Album* is a more comic book since it gives its reader the comedy of the human condition.

Laughter Against

If *The Thurber Album* laughs in celebration of the vitality and meanings in its nineteenth-century human beings, Thurber uses his comedy to laugh against debilitating forces in life in his collections of sketches written at the same time. We all fear laughter

against us if our manners or speech are not quite right or our dress
is peculiar. In *Thurber Country* (1953) and *Lanterns and Lances*
(1961) laughter is directed against behaviors that must be scourged,
the familiar love of power, familiar stupidity, and familiar inaccuracy of speech and thought. In his last collections, Thurber scolds
with laughter small-brained men, dumb critics, and our national
mania to seize on solutions drawn from special and limited studies
of human behavior. His laughter is directed against specialists
who see life from one little dimension, from one little niche, instead
of the whole and steady vision of the nineteenth-century men and
women like Jacob Fisher or Aunt Margery Albright.

The Master's touch is still evident in these last essays and
stories when Thurber dramatizes his enemy rather than making
a frontal attack on the malaise. Among the stories in *Thurber
Country*-where the touch is striking and profound is "Teacher's
Pet." The struggle of this story is between a weak man of intelligence and a strong man of physical prowess: the story calls it
a struggle between a teacher's pet and a shot-putter. The hero
Willber Kelby is another example of Walter Mitty or Erwin Martin.
Opposed to Willber Kelby is Bob Stevenson, a new incarnation of
the ex-football player from Pittsburgh in *The Male Animal*. On
the familiar melody, however, Thurber manages to play a new and
striking variation. The confrontation this time is intensified by
Kelby's recent intimation of mortality:

> [Kelby] had had, the day before, something very like a religious
> experience, of a darkly ominous nature. It had been brought
> on by his reading a magazine article dealing with the fears and
> neurotic disturbances of the human male in middle age. Kelby
> was three months past fifty, and the article had upset him, par-
> ticularly in its reference to the sometimes disastrous shock
> caused by the aging man's recognition of the fact of death, the
> inevitability of his perhaps not too distant termination. Women,
> the article intimated, were better adjusted to the certainty of
> extinction and rarely gave it a conscious thought, but a man in
> his fifties or later — often earlier — might be stricken all of a sudden
> by the realization of impending death, with serious nervous or
> even mental sequelae.
>
> Kelby had wondered, putting the magazine down, if the dread
> experience had come to him in his forties, say, and he had for-
> gotten it.

The tone is comic; Kelby fears that he has missed a major experience in life and we laugh at him for suspecting that he could.

This story, however, varies not only in its intimation of death but also in its resolution. Had the story been written in the 1930's or early 1940's, Thurber might have ended it with the hero leaving the scene with a whimper, but in this story the hero experiences an ironic but apparent triumph in his action. At the suburban cocktail party where the confrontation between intelligence and power occurs, Willber Kelby talks to a female neighbor whose son Elbert is a teacher's pet. The conversation occurs because of the appearance of Bob Stevenson, Jr., a younger version of his father. At the end of the story (and a day later), Willber Kelby finds young Stevenson on the street hazing Elbert. Kelby, stung by the memory of his own persecution as a teacher's pet, strikes the young incarnation of himself! He does not strike young Stevenson. He strikes the teacher's pet. When Bob Stevenson, Sr., hears the story, he calls Willber Kelby a bully. The story exploits the same awareness Thurber uses in *The Thurber Album,* the awareness of the disjunction between intelligence and power. Kelby, like the newspapermen and the teachers, is nearly impotent himself, but he strikes Elbert in an effort to give the child the kind of challenge which encouraged the solid American characters of the past to respond to their world and thus discover their "bright and separate values." Kelby's gesture may be futile, but it is an act; he is not content to dream, like Walter Mitty. His story has an ironic comic triumph when Stevenson so grossly misreads the action. The reader senses a further irony, for in the story the intelligence descends to the sin it fights; the reader is thus once more aware of the catastrophic stage upon which the comedy is acted. Kelby's victory is pyrrhic since the comfortable world of Bob Stevenson cannot comprehend the victory. Stevenson does not have the intelligence to get beyond the obvious; he will not explore as Mr. Ziegfeld, Aunt Margery Albright, or Mary Agnes Thurber explore the surface of action to discover meaning. In our jumpy time, the story says, we jump to the obvious and not to meaning.

The story is a fine piece of writing and worthy, I think, of comparison to Mitty. "The Secret Life of Walter Mitty" differs from "Teacher's Pet" just as *My Life and Hard Times* differs from *The Thurber Album.* In both cases the earlier version is funnier, if we judge merely on laughter, because the earlier version exploits comic types more fully. The second story gives us laughter and awareness of a human pain and victory. The gods on Olympus must see the world so fully and so surely.

Lesser pieces in the final four collections exploit observable human situations. In *Alarms and Diversions,* for example, a sketch entitled "Get Thee to a Monastery" laments the power of young actresses and laughs at the success these young women have in seducing theater-goers and critics to forget the play or its ideas. "The Moribundant Life, or Grow Old Along with Whom?" in the same collection treats the strange inability of American writers to live long and productive lives, and concludes that their powerful and misdirected world grinds them to their graves sooner than other writers. Lamentations over the state of language in these last books regret that intelligence in statement has completely succumbed to Madison Avenue and laziness. Thurber concludes, in one of his morose pieces, "Life at the moment is a tale told in an idiom, full of unsoundness and fury signifying nonism." In "The New Vocabularianism," from *Lanterns and Lances,* he worries about efforts to simplify and thus reduce meaning in language. "The brain," he writes, "is. . .made up largely of potassium, phosphorus, propaganda, and politics." Two files of letters in *Thurber Country,* one with a publisher's office and another with customs officials, illustrate once more that the world pays little attention to language or action. The recipients of Thurber's letters put their own meaning into his words or else get so involved in procedure that the human question is totally lost. In "The Psychosemanticist Will See You Now, Mr. Thurber," he concludes with a cause for his malaise; the world is full of bumblers and "the bumbler is spared the tedious exercising of his mental faculties." In these sketches the laughter is overt; the shot-putter Bob Stevenson type is an obvious subject for ridicule and the Thurber-Kelby figures are distant enough so that laughter provides a release from pity at the sight of so much pain. We can laugh even at the fierce parody of Goldsmith's "Deserted Village": "Ill fares the land, to galloping fears a prey, where gobbledy-gook accumulates and words decay." His comedy blasts the misdirected and it hopes for a better use of mental power.

The fault needing correction is not just in ordinary men but in those who see themselves as men of intellect. Thurber puts himself and his own reputation at hazard in that astonishing tour de force, "The Tyranny of Trivia" (in *Lanterns and Lances*) mentioned earlier. The reader will recall that the critic, Otto Friedrich, had been "distressed to discover that [Thurber's work] had been ravaged by trivia." The critic had leapt to an obvious conclusion. He admits the charge and then plays into the jaws of the attack by writing ten pages of results from the everlasting word games that he plays with himself to keep from "talking back to the wallpaper." When he is a patient in a hospital, he tries to play his game with his nurses (the apotheosis of dulled, overworked, prosaic twentieth-century society), but the nurses summon physicians and avoid the game. The physicians are also unable to answer Thurber's word challenges, and thus Thurber is left to himself — in trivia. But is he? The joke is on the intrepid critic who thinks that he has found another example to illustrate his thesis. Thurber's fascination with words and their patterns (he discovers the frightful combination of the letters C and M in Capulet and Montague, and Capitalism and Marxism) is at once the glory of the human mind and the remembrance of primitive man's conviction that the name and the thing are so closely related that one cannot say the name without invoking the object. Primitive man may appear naive, but unless modern man can connect the word and the object, then his thought is mere bombast and propaganda. In Thurber's word game, the reader is once more astounded by the inventive possibilities of the imagination that finds even in trivia the meaning and distinction of the human experience. The dull symbols of our century, the nurses and physicians, are lost in the chaos of words just like the Royal Wizards in the children's stories. The artist, however, discovers meaning. Thurber invents to show, ostensibly, how far he has descended into trivia, but his invention shows, in fact, how the human mind finds order even in a dictionary. The mind, he dares to show us, is more than phosphorus, potassium and propaganda, for it is a creative agent.

The subject of Thurber's laughter is our tendency to seize upon any floating idea and translate it into sudden and unholy panaceas. The most fearsome threat is the specialist (like the critic finding trivia) who limits himself to one aspect of experience. Thurber has laughed at such specialization in marriage counsellors (in *Is Sex Necessary?*) and in psychologists (in *Let Your Mind Alone*). In "The Last Clock: A Fable for the Time, Such as It Is, of Man" in *Lanterns and Lances,* Thurber returns once more to the method of the fables and the method of his stories for children to dramatize the threat of specialism. The fable tells of an ogre who "had fallen into the habit of eating clocks." He eats all but one of the clocks in his town before his death because no one can help the poor suffering addict. Specialists try to ease his agony, but specialists can only prescribe according to previous training, and no one has seen a clock-eater before. Clockmen, clogmen, a general practitioner (he treats only generals), psychochronologists, and clockonomists try to help the addict, but they all fail. In the fable Thurber shows dramatically what he states directly in "The Future, if Any, of Comedy" in *Credos and Curios:*

> We are divided into literally hundreds of Area Men, none of whom knows or cares very much about men in other categories of endeavor or thought. But we mumble along in our multiple confusion. Every man is now an island unto himself, interested in, even obsessed by, his own preoccupation.

In the fable, the ogre finally dies of his disease because the Area Men are totally inadequate to the new disease. They cannot see beyond their clichés.

Thurber is not finished with his fable. One clock remains in the town, but the modern plague still grinds to its own unconscionable conclusion. A final specialist, a collector, demands that the last clock be allowed to run down and be placed in a museum. The Supreme Magistrate cannot see well enough to deny the rule "that the last clock is a collector's item, or museum piece," and therefore he sends it to the museum. As in Thurber's stories for children, time dies and the society dies. A thousand years later travelers from Venus find the clock in the desert that has covered it, but they cannot identify it because the town inspirationalist (the debased form of the poet) forgot the name of the object when he made out the museum card. Thurber in this fable makes us laugh at a catastrophic society. He exaggerates our penchant to reduce our vision of human experience and become specialists who can see and judge only in small areas of experience. Life is larger than the rational mind—the mind of the psychochronologist or clockonomists—and Thurber excoriates our reductionism. The tendency is potentially tragic, but in laughing at it, Thurber directs his world toward more human ideals, and gives his reader much pleasure in allowing him to laugh against the danger of such foolishness.

In Thurber's late sketches the anger at the graying mass cannot always be contained within a dramatic vision. He states his fears nakedly and directly and thus becomes a specialist himself. Just as Willber Kelby, he falls into the clutches of what he would fight. That he knows his own foolishness is clear from the story entitled "The Interview" in *Thurber Country*. In the story, three previous attempts by others having failed, a fourth newspaperman tries to interview a successful author of eighteen books. The interview, however, degenerates into a list of the author's savage peeves against his world: stereotyped social conversations, the inability of newspapers to quote accurately, women authors who see the world through the sensitive eyes of ten-year-old moppets, the invasion of privacy. All of the peeves appear somewhere in Thurber's own eighteen books. After his seventh or eighth drink, the distinguished author says that he has always wanted to cut a dove open to look for omens and "go crying through the night, like another Whozis, 'Repent, ye sinners, repent. The world is coming to an end.'" Like the author of *Ecclesiastes* and like Thurber himself in some of his late essays, the distinguished author rages against the dying of the light in his society. The story is full of comic vitality and it ends, significantly, with the sound of his voice bawling the names of three of his four wives in the further recesses of the house. Although the reporter leaves the house with no story, his failure is a comic victory. He cannot write a story saying that the self destroys itself raging against its enemy. Our laughter at the confused reporter and our laughter at the distinguished author crying his vitality is contained within a dramatic framework of action, but the story points toward Thurber's own behavior in some of his final pieces. This story too recalls Henry James, for like James in "Death of a Lion," it laughs and cries at the position of the artist in society. The artist is a misfit, a jester, a mere device. The reporters get no story because to get a story would be to acquiesce to what society and the self have done to Thurber's writer. Ordinary mortals will not see. Neither James nor Thurber indulges in a facile romanticism to say that the writer must suffer, but he does suffer because he is sensitive enough to see what we gloss over. The balance between rage at error and recognition in this story is one of Thurber's greatest achievements. We can laugh at the same time that we recognize.

In less successful sketches and essays Thurber embarrasses his reader just as the distinguished author embarrasses the reporter. *Credos and Curios*, for example, includes elegies and lamentations, prefaces and comments that Thurber wrote for dead friends. They are often painful, without the release of laughter, because they state directly. As a character comments in one of the final stories, "The Danger in the House," Thurber has "given up discussion for oration."

The comic writer has insisted often that his comedy purges society of evils and articulates the general will of mankind. His task was easier (or seems easier to us) in the past when society had a general will clearly stated by Church, State, University, and the governing class. Thurber's general will is harder to state since it is an attitude rather than a system of values. The only thing we have in the way of a general will is a strong desire for ease, comfort, pleasure, release—the very subject of Thurber's attack. To counter the threat, Thurber offers a mind that energetically penetrates to discover sense and meaning. A method of mind is a weak power; it is no wonder that Thurber loses faith and turns to raging within the further recesses of the house.

Laughter Transformed

Now, *The Years with Ross* seems an inevitable book, a final statement of all Thurber's themes. Ross is the perfect Thurber subject, seen often in partial form in earlier books but now cohering from the fragments. Thurber says that King Clode in *The White Deer* was unconsciously modeled on Ross. Ross-like characters appear in "The Waters of the Moon" (*The Beast in Me*) and "The Cane in the Corridor" (*The Thurber Carnival*). The many practical jokers in Thurber sketches may be traced to Ross since he was a consummate practical joker. If the distinguished author of eighteen books in "The Interview" has the irascibility

of Thurber, he also has the imperviousness and single minded-
ness of Ross, and only one more wife than Ross himself. Ross
is not, it goes almost without saying, the little Thurber man pat-
iently filing, driving, or worrying in the shadow of some vital
woman; he is, rather, Walter Mitty in triumph. Thurber's fascination with the man as a potential subject is clear from the fact
that he attempted to write a play on Ross in 1948. Ross also recalls Thurber's relatives in the early part of *The Thurber Album.*
Like them, he has intelligence and vitality. Thurber makes the
connection explicit when he compares Ross to his mother and to
Gus Kuehner, Thurber's editor in Columbus. Ross is, however,
of a different breed than Keuhner, for Ross continued to grow
(like Thurber's mother) and to grow as the challenge he faced
developed. Ross has what Kuehner did not have: the ability to
make and to impose his meaning like the jesters and poets in Thurber's books for children. Although the biography of Ross ends
with a death scene, the reader feels—just as surely as in the marriage scenes at the end of the books for children—a sense of comic
triumph.

Since *The Years with Ross* brings together so much in Thurber's
other work, nothing in Thurber can stand comparison to the book.
The most useful comparison, it seems to me, is to compare Ross
with Prince Hal in Shakespeare's two *Henry IV* plays. The comparison has the kind of literary-ness that Ross, as Thurber makes
clear, would object to, but the comparison is apt and useful. In
the first place, as in Shakespeare's plays, we watch a hero confronting odds that are inescapable. Prince Hal obtains the victories of an ideal hero, as Ross does, but his victories are pyrrhic
since the action begun in the plays, as Shakespeare's audience
well knew, ends in the tragedy of the War of Roses. Prince Hal,
then, acts before a curtain of a catastrophic society. Ross too has
a pyrrhic victory, for we well know that a union of power, intelligence, patience, and discipline is a fragile coalition apt to dis-
integrate. Ross's passion for accuracy, his interest in (and exempli-
fication of) distinction, and his power of creative intelligence run
counter to the apparent will of mass society and mass culture.
Like the odds against Hal, the odds against Ross were tremendous
and the chief wonder is that he did succeed. Thus, as our pleasure
in Hal's victory is enhanced by our knowledge of a coming defeat,

so our pleasure in Ross's success is enhanced by our knowledge of the force against him.

> [Ross] had been a great success, he had made hundreds of friends and thousands of admirers, he had contributed something that had not happened before in this country, or anywhere else, to literature, comedy, and journalism, and he was leaving behind him an imposing monument. He had got his frail weekly off the rocky shoals of 1925 and piloted it into safe harbor through Depression and Recession, World War II, and the even greater perils of the McCarthy era. His good ship stood up all the way. He sometimes threatened to quit, and he was at least twice threatened with being fired, but he kept on going like a bullet-torn battle flag, and nobody captured his colors and nobody silenced his drums.

He is as fitting a hero as Prince Hal, for the ideal he represents faced a strong foe and won—if only for a moment.

Thurber's words for the obstacles recall another aspect of *The Years with Ross* that invites comparison to Shakespeare's plays about Hal. Shakespeare's history plays are a full scale review of English society at the dawn of the Renaissance. *The Years with Ross* also has epic qualities since the story of Ross's work ranges across a large area of American intellectual life during the first half of the twentieth century. Ross knew everyone, Thurber says, "from Groucho Marx to Lord Dalhousie." Ross was "like a show, or a pageant, or a monument, or a movement." Like Prince Hal, Ross is larger than life and legendary (Thurber's book sets the legend down in its true gospel to correct two earlier versions of Ross's story). And further Ross experienced the three great traumatic shocks of the first half of the century—the First World War, the Depression, and the Second World War with its terrible aftermath. In a time when genuine heroes are rare, Ross is as close as we can come to knowing a true Odysseus in our time.

Thurber divides the story of Ross into sixteen chapters, each of which may be read as a separate essay (they were published first in the *Atlantic Monthly*), but a better way to understand the book is to recognize that it falls into five major parts. The first part (the first three chapters) describes Ross's slow discovery of himself. The second part (chapters four and five) considers Ross in repose; he talks to Mencken and Nathan and works with his own staff on "The Talk of the Town." This section is quiet, with little drama. The third section (chapters six, seven, and eight) is a history of the *New Yorker;* Ross seeks a miracle man as managing editor and gradually expands the magazine's range from a city publication to a national voice. The fourth section (chapters nine to fourteen) shows Ross responding to sex, money, legal problems, cocktail parties, and automobiles — the trivia of modern man. The final section (the final two chapters) juxtaposes Ross and Alexander Woollcott. Giving Woollcott the penultimate chapter (he appears only briefly in the book up to this point) enables Thurber to dramatize Ross's vitality and allows the conventional lamentations on death to fall on Woollcott so that Ross's own end is triumphant.

In the first section of Thurber's book Ross is in training and acquiring the staff of writers that gave the magazine its initial tone. The first chapter on the art meetings held every Tuesday afternoon shows the dialectic of mind that produces the *New Yorker's* first success, its art. Although Ross makes incredible mistakes (he tried to make Thurber an editor and he fired his best managing editor), he learns from the mistakes so that his own drive and power combine with a growing understanding and intelligence. He discovers the texture, clarity, and purpose of the magazine and his own method. Although this first part is interesting because it describes the seeds which Ross and the magazine will develop, it is no more interesting than any other attempt to treat a successful man. Ross is, in this opening section, a mortal and not a hero.

The second part, the section that looks at Ross in repose, examines the mind that Ross brought to his task. On the surface that mind is not particularly promising. The nearest comparison to him is Aunt Margery Albright who also, from all outward appearances, has little to offer. Thurber calls Ross a "Gee Whiz guy," an unsophisticated westerner, an innocent, an American. He comes to his job, the reader feels, with only a drive to construct and the skill to manipulate printing schedules. His general reading is "like a trip into darkest Confusia, without a map." His mind is "uncluttered by culture." He knows nothing about music, philosophy, or poetry. He once asks whether Moby Dick is the whale or the man. His little knowledge is from dictionaries and Fowler's

A Dictionary of Modern English Usage; the only thing he reads is
his own magazine. Like Aunt Margery, he lacks specialist's training,
but he has an uncanny knack of acquiring intelligence and growing
as the demands are placed on him. He complains to Thurber that
"Nobody has any self-discipline," but quite evidently Ross does.
Like Aunt Margery, Ross has the patience to wait and the self-
discipline to discover. Because his mind is uncluttered by culture
with its preconceptions, he is a natural man. Keats said that poetry
should come as the leaves of the tree or it should not come at all;
to Ross editing comes as naturally as the leaves to a tree. Thurber
broods "about the mystery. . .of. . .the central paradox of Harold
Ross's nature; that is, his magic gift of surrounding himself with
some of the best talent in America, despite his own literary and
artistic limitations." Ross has a mind so fine, as T. S. Eliot described the mind of Henry James, that it is not damaged by a single
idea. Like Aunt Margery, Ross simply does his job and attracts
to himself the talent and genius that he does because he learns
to consider only the immediate in his world of experience. Thurber's comedy has always tried to state the idea that Ross practiced: that man understands his universe best who judges the universe by his own intelligence rather than by abstract intellect. In
this sense he is like Thurber's women who are unruffled by ideas
and other distractions. Ross has an instinctive intelligence that
is like instinct in animals; his intelligence works to shape and
form without the crippling freight of prejudice or abstract ideas
about what a magazine ought to be. Or, to put it another way,
Thurber in this section of his book shows that Ross is uncontami-
nated with major premises; thus his mind inductively shapes
meaning out of experience.

The third section of Thurber's book is a history of Ross and
his magazine growing into maturity. Out of the friction of Ross
positive and Ross negative a hero and a monument develop. The
major idea of this section is the same that concerns Thurber in so
many of his sketches and stories in his last four collections: the
idea of accuracy and care. It is no surprise to learn of Ross that
"He was meticulous to the point of obsession about the appearance
of his magazine." He dreamed of perfection, and he was never
satisfied by any near approach. "Ross hired anybody, and every-
body, in his frantic and ceaseless search for the Fountain of Per-

fection. . . . [The] quest itself was what kept him going." Ralph Ingersoll, Thurber writes, "was the best of all the Central Desk men, the very administrative expert Ross spent his life looking for," but Ingersoll's tenure was not notably longer than that of some of the other men who tried to serve Ross in his frantic desire to realize what he alone saw. The "harried old perfectionist" tries every idea like a scientist in a laboratory testing hypotheses in hope that each one might add something to the grand formula that he seeks.

The fourth section looks at Ross as a human being, and again the reader is aware of the paradox of his personality. Ross refuses to be reduced to any abstract generalization. Although he edits a sophisticated magazine, Ross is not a sophisticated man. A secretary robs him of $71,000; as Thurber comments, "It takes a really great eccentric to be robbed of seventy-one thousand dollars right under his busy nose." In whatever setting Ross appears in these chapters, whether gambling or preparing his attack on the Luce publications, his distinction and drive are apparent. He is always startling; he has a "virtual inability to talk without a continous flow of profanity" but he spells out euphemisms in front of women. Wherever we see him he has his own bright, separate values.

The last two chapters discuss Alexander Woollcott and Ross's final years. Woollcott is both a Hotspur and Falstaff to Ross. Like Hotspur, he has an exaggerated sense of his own honor and position. Like Falstaff he is a fat buffoon. Woollcott's infertility, his narcissism, his exhibitionism contrast with Ross's masculinity, Ross's interest in others, and Ross's desire to remain behind the scenes. Although Thurber treats Woollcott respectfully, he makes Woollcott's essential sterility clear. Ross said Woollcott "thinks he knows more about everything that happens than anybody else. He only knows a few things, and he tells them over and over." Ross catches Woollcott once with almost identical articles in the *New Yorker* and *McCall's.* Thurber quotes Gibbs as saying, "I guess [Woollcott] was one of the most dreadful writers who ever existed." His narcissism is seen in Ross's comment that at his famous Sunday morning breakfasts, Woollcott "sits there like a fat duchess holding her dirty rings to be kissed." Thurber theorizes that Woollcott "was the Grand Marshal of a perpetual pageant, pompous in demeanor, riding a high horse, wearing the medals of his own peculiar punctilio and perfectionism." His exhibitionism appears in his costumes and in his writing. But Woollcott is the man who should, abstractly, have the wit, the learning, the experience, the attitude, and the intelligence to edit the *New Yorker*, yet he is in fact, petty, vindictive, and ineffectual. The relationship between them is expressed in the parody cover of the anniversary issue of the *New Yorker;* the face of Ross is put on the figure of the nineteenth-century dandy and Woollcott is the butterfly "he is examining contemptuously." Woollcott is the apotheosis of all that Thurber's comedy ridicules and attacks. He represents both the comfort, ease, and conventionality of Mrs. Mitty and the misguided meddling intellect of the marriage counsellors and the psychologists; he is the obtuseness of Bob Stevenson and the men of affairs that so easily crush the Thurber hero in the 1930's. Although he has intellect, Woollcott lacks imagination, the ability to wrest from experience a fresh and direct comprehension of its significance.

Ross is the very opposite of Woollcott. He is capable of love and kindness; he has not inherited taste but he has learned truth. He does not act to make an impression, but he acts to accomplish his task. In the gallery of Thurber subjects after the books for children, Ross is the only man who has a comic triumph, the vital surge of energy that springs from the tensions and contradictions of his own being. Even in his death, he is alive.

In Ross's victory, we are aware of the catastrophic society around him. Ross, however, has the dedicated energy to transform it; "He was always in mid-flight, or on the edge of his chair, alighting or about to take off." Because of his energy, he beats down his own business department with its advice of prudence and caution. He succeeds in creating a magazine that the sensible world would never have asked for if it had been given the chance to ask. Although his magazine makes money, the purpose of the magazine remains true; it does not, like others, become a non-magazine, a vehicle to carry advertising. Ross constantly fears that he and his magazine will fall into a formula. He has the courage to fight McCarthyism. He urges, cajoles, and bullies his creative men to produce because the world needs their imaginative insight. The success that Ross enjoys is impressive because of the odds against him. Were the odds not so large, his story would interest no one. Not only does the book provide a sense of triumph, the standard need of comedy, but it also provides the reader with a full sense of the unsound and fuzzy obstacles pitted against the hero. We sense not only victory but obstacle. In such comedy Thurber reaches the full invention of a comic artist: to see not only the victory but the chaos from which the victory springs.

The book on Ross fittingly climaxes Thurber's career. In it his comedy fulfills the positive social use of the form. In the 1930's Kenneth Burke complained about Thurber and all comedy because the comic artist bends everything in his power to get laughter. Burke could not, I think, make the same complaint about *The Years with Ross* or *The Thurber Album*. In these books, and in other sketches that Thurber wrote in his last decade, the reader understands a full human experience that is at the same moment both particular and universal. Thurber's skill as a writer and his advantage as a participant insure that the particular quality of Ross's personality and of the personality of the men and women in the *Album* is full before our sight. He makes us see.

That *The Years with Ross* achieves the universal is evident from the extent to which Thurber exploits the standard techniques of comedy. The book plays appearances against reality: the home-spun country boy trained in the gut-fighting of newspaper journalism in reality proves to be a successful editor serving a civilization. Ross is caught in the unconscious bondage or continuation that marks the comic figure; just as surely as Jimmy Durante's nose is funny, Ross's phrases "Done and Done" or "Well, God bless you, goddam it," are funny. So also Ross's single minded determination is comic. He is thoroughly unconscious of himself; he will, despite all evidence that the reader knows, try to make an editor out of James M. Cain and James Thurber. The impostors that threaten Ross, from Alexander Woollcott to the men in his business office, are genuine impostors who threaten not just the hero but the human condition. Because his opposition is worthy and serious, our laughter is genuine pleasure. Finally Ross has the vital energy of the comic hero. Thurber quotes a London friend who comments on meeting Ross, "During the first half hour. . . . I felt that Ross was the last man in the world who could edit the *New Yorker*. I left there realizing nobody else in the world could."

He is a natural power. In his story the reader experiences the cleansing satisfaction of seeing a struggle and a victory, of seeing excellence triumph over error that needs correction and amendment. From the story we acquire a sense of proportion or understanding about the world we live in. The book, therefore, supplies a rich comic understanding of the human condition—here, the condition of one of our heroes, Ross.

I said at the beginning of this chapter that Thurber's admirers scanned every work in his final decade with trepidation. Comedy, we think, is a young man's art since only the young man has the energy and drive to establish the reformed society that typically begins when the comedy ends. The classical end of comedy, a marriage, symbolizes the new society and the regeneration implicit in the action. Since the comic character needs energy, we fear that the older writer cannot have the energy to establish his comic view. The fear is especially strong for Thurber's readers since so many of his late pieces treat the subject of age in American writers who burn out young. Thurber's final comedy succeeds because his sense of form persists in his shift from a stereotyped comedy to a comedy of human action. The unsound and fuzzy impostors threatening in Thurber's final books are not constructions but facts of human experience just as the impostors in primitive comedy represent natural forces in the world which threaten to destroy humanity. His heroes are not artfully created men but rather existential heroes, men who have the power to form the chaotic world of experience into meaning. The comedy of Ross and the men and women like Jacob Fisher and Aunt Margery Albright is a comedy of seeing things as they really are, a comedy of finding in experience itself the ritual action of challenge, defeat, despair, and final victory. While the action often ends in death, the spirit of his heroes survives. His comedy therefore is a human comedy (rather than a divine comedy), and it gives his readers a very human revelation of a very human and transitory *Paradiso.*

IX

The Art
of James Thurber

Poems, W. H. Auden says, are either Ariel poems which delight by their sheer beauty or Prospero poems which impress us because of their instruction or truth, but the ideal poem perfectly balances the two impulses. Thurber's truth or instruction can be stated in the form of general ideas and compared to other experiences, but the quality of delight is much more difficult to describe. One tends to run off into uncertain words like *magic*, or *pleasure*, or *delight*. Taste is an individual possession and a writer's art is a gossamer web that shatters easily; I can show that "The Day the Dam Broke" strikes sympathetic chords in the mind that knows what happened at Munich much more easily than I can specify precisely what causes delight.

To prove Thurber an artist (a word he never uses except to describe painters or cartoonists), I measure him by the fact that he creates a clear, complete, and recognizable world or vision. Within that world, he creates in his reader's mind an expectation or tension. Since the expectation or tension has relevance to ordinary human experience, it engages the reader (a point which I take up again for this new focus). The tension is resolved so that it thoroughly satisfies. Finally, in arriving at Thurber's resolution, the reader recognizes a power of language, a sense of the way that words communicate and delight. Malcolm Cowley says that Thurber's words "give the impression of standing cleanly and separately on the page, each in its place like stones in a well-built wall." Within the range of comedy, Cowley goes on to say, nobody writes better than Thurber, "that is, more clearly and flexibly, with a deeper feeling for the genius of the language and the value of the words." See *Works Consulted.* I would like to examine the texture of Thurber's well-built wall that merits Cowley's praise.

His World

The musician learns to recognize Mozart's music without formal identification because Mozart writes in predictable ways. Mozart may be full of infinite variety, but we recognize always a familiar stance. The qualities that mark a musician or a writer may be called his style, but I prefer to call it his world. Thurber's world is marked by its intensity of concentration, by its distance from ordinary events, and by a characteristic that has been called, inaccurately, Freudian. Other qualities distinguish Thurber, but these three will serve as a beginning to define provisionally his special view. With only these three, I could not identify for certain a Thurber sketch published without his name, but these three support the other qualities that mark his world.

Thurber writes from an interior view of human experience that is sometimes so private as to be embarrassing. Husbands argue with wives late in the night; an entire sketch may be spoken by Thurber lying in a hospital bed or sitting in a bar contemplating the antic behavior of unknown persons. The sketches report secret lives. His problem as a writer is to cross the barrier between his perception and the reader's experience; he must join interior experience with exterior understanding. His method differs from that of his contemporaries Yeats, Eliot, and Joyce for they connect their interior vision with ideas of Byzantium, grail myths, or the Odyssey. Thurber crosses the barrier by writing of generalized types: husbands, lonely men in cities, servant women. He reduces his action to the basic form of comedy: a witty man facing the imponderable obstacles of chance and fortune and yet triumphing over them. He also externalizes his vision by placing his action in a past that is far enough away to be removed from ordinary feelings but near enough to be recognizable. Even in contemporary settings, Thurber rarely ties his action to known phenomena or events. Thus instead of writing about Senator McCarthy in "The Glass of Fashion," he writes about a general congressional investigation. His cocktail parties take place in Suburbia or in a City rather than a particular suburb in Connecticut or on a particular street in New York. The key to his method—a method of both intensity and distance—is reported by Thurber himself when he prints a remark that a producer made about a play Thurber wrote:

> A dozen years ago [i.e. in 1948] I began writing a play about Ross and the *New Yorker*, a comedy whose three acts took place in the art room. When I showed the first draft of Act I to a famous man of the Broadway theater he said, "I have a sense of isolation about that meeting room, as if the characters were marooned there and there was nobody else in the building. There must have been people in the other offices on the floor, but I don't feel them."

The statement applies to all of Thurber's best writing; the activities in Columbus or Connecticut are isolated and complete. The neighbors never intrude except to become part of the world. In this isolated, bounded, and intense world Thurber obtains objectivity without the need for racial myth (which may be arbitrary) such as Yeats or Eliot uses. The same forces that move in our ordinary world of experience also move in the intense, isolated world that Thurber creates, but in Thurber's world, they move disinterestedly and more truly (because they are more separated from chance and accident) than in our world or even in the interior world where Thurber first saw them.

Thurber distills from the accidents of chance and chaos essential forces and sets these forces into action in his world. Ross is *not* like Odysseus or Prometheus or Prince Hal; he is Ross, a unique man, but we see him truly and fully removed from the chance events that surround ordinary life. He stands in relation to our experience in the same way that Prometheus, Odysseus, or Prince Hal stand in relation to the world of experience in which they originally existed. Because of the stripping, Ross becomes a universal figure. At his death we do not feel despair that a good man has died and the gray mass has claimed one more victim; rather, we feel joy that this man lived so well despite the odds. If we define the artist as the man who omits, then Thurber, the artist, omits everything that is temporal or accidental about Ross so that we can see the single and intense figure of Ross standing out above his society, representing it and transcending it. The same may be said about Walter Mitty, Mr. Monroe, or Willber Kelby.

Another aspect of Thurber's world endlessly noticed by reviewers is the fact that it could not exist without Freud. The comment is informative since so much of Thurber's world is that seen from inside the unconscious that Freud teaches us to recognize. "One is a Wanderer" in *The Middle-Aged Man on the Flying Trapeze* tells the secret of a desperately lonely man. In "The Remarkable Case of Mr. Bruhl" in the same collection, Mr. Bruhl's personality disintegrates because he happens to look like a notorious criminal. Since these men act in patterns that their rational, conscious minds cannot fathom, I can see that Freud has helped the reader to understand them. Thurber makes the same discovery that Freud did when Freud, according to Lionel Trilling, "showed us that poetry is indigenous to the very constitution of the mind" (See *Works Consulted*). Thurber's comedy repeatedly grows out of the very constitution of the mind, from the constitution of Grandfather's mind in *My Life and Hard Times* to the constitution of Aunt Margery Albright's mind in *The Thurber Album*.

The discovery of unconscious movements of events shaping man and his attitudes is found in another writer that Thurber admires (Thurber was appalled by Freud). Wordsworth ranks second behind Henry James as the writer Thurber most frequently invokes and parodies. In *The Prelude*, his long autobiographical poem, Wordsworth seeks lugubriously what Thurber seeks comically in *My Life and Hard Times*. Wordsworth writes (1850, I, 340-50),

> the immortal spirit grows
> Like harmony in music; there is a dark
> Inscrutable workmanship that reconciles
> Discordant elements, makes them cling together
> In one society. How strange that all
> The terrors, pains, and early miseries,
> Regrets, vexations, lassitudes interfused
> Within my mind, should e'er have born a part,
> And that a needful part, in making up

The calm existence that is mine when I
Am worthy of myself.

In these lines Wordsworth, pondering the mystery that shapes the imagination, names the experiences that shaped his imagination. Thurber, in the passage from *My Life* quoted earlier, explains how his imagination was shaped by a wild roller-coaster ride during the last days of the First World War:

> That trip, although it ended safely, made a lasting impression on me. It is not too much to say that it has flavored my life. It is the reason I shout in my sleep, refuse to ride on the elevated. keep jerking the emergency brake in cars other people are driving, have the sensation of flying like a bird when I first lie down, and in certain months can't keep anything on my stomach.

Like Wordsworth, Thurber describes the "Discordant elements. . . in terrors, pains, and early miseries" that make life significant and meaningful. Thurber's method is Wordsworthian not only in the autobiographical books like *My Life and Hard Times, The Thurber Album,* or *The Years with Ross,* but also in cocktail party sketches that invite us to wonder why people behave as they do, in word game sketches that find the "inscrutable workmanship" in language, and in stories of interior terror like "The Whip-Poor-Will." It is not that Thurber is post-Freudian; he is post-Wordsworthian.

A third special quality of Thurber's comic world is the fact that, following Wordsworth, meaningful action takes place within the human personality. Even in the story of Ross, a man who does act in the catastrophic world, our attention is directed toward the inner man. If the word were not unfashionable, I would say that Thurber gives us victories of the spirit. The victory that Walter Mitty knows is known only to Mitty, and it is a victory only in the frame of his own experience and values. When Erwin Martin defeats Mrs. Ulgine Barrows, he cannot even smile at his victory, for if he betrays the slightest hint of his successful ruse, his whole victory will turn to ashes. The readers, granted, share with the hero; they have been through the experience with him and have learned the truths that will make his victories possible. Only in the world of their values is the victory complete.

Comedies end with dances of celebration. In the bawdy celebration at the end of a play by Aristophanes all nature is dancing. In the ballet at the end of a Molière comedy all society is dancing. To Aristophanes and Molière nature and society share with man a common system of values so that all may celebrate. Thurber's dance is a dance of the spirit and the melody is within the dancer. In Thurber only the hero and the percipient reader know the real truth and victory for only the hero knows the values upon which the victory has been won. The stories for children are an exception since they end with a public victory, but even in them, the poets and jesters obtain their victory by the power of their imaginations to impose order. To adapt the Cartesian formula, Thurber's characters say, our thinking triumphs and therefore we are.

The Tension in Thurber's World

The battle between men and women is so pervasive in Thurber that one can hardly believe it is not a natural subject for all comic writers since Aristophanes' *Lysistrata*. As a matter of fact, the battle is not a usual subject at all; women are, typically, the prize awarded to the hero and they may play a subsidiary role in the comedy, but they do not often participate in the action. In *The Thurber Album*, for example, Aunt Margery Albright (a novelist could hardly invent a better name) struggles with a modern scientific nurse; the prize in this contest (a complete reversal of normal patterns) is Thurber's own father who is, according to Aunt Margery, being badly nursed:

> The meeting between the starched young lady in white and the bent old woman in black was the meeting of the present and the past, the newfangled and the old-fashioned, the ritualistic and the instinctive, and the shock of antagonistic schools of thought clashing sent out cold sparks. Miss Wilson was coolly disdainful, and Mrs. Albright plainly hated her crisp guts. . . . All the rest of her life, Aunt Margery, recalling the scene that followed, would mimic Miss Wilson's indignation, crying in a shrill voice, "It shan't be done!" waving a clenched fist in the air, exaggerating the young nurse's wrath. "It shan't be done!" she would repeat, relaxing at last with a clutch at her protesting kneecap and a satisfied smile.

The scene could be inserted into a philosophic work on comedy describing its archetypal form. Thank God Thurber knew nothing about the comic plot I have talked about so much, for he could not have written the scene if he had been conscious of what he was saying. He transcribed the human condition, and, welling up in that condition, is the old ritual of mankind. Yet, curiously, inside the old ritual or tradition is a new, delightful, and very serious addition to the ritual: the female opponent.

Thurber's women are not all large, bossy, restrictive, and reductionist imposters like Miss Wilson; many of them are comic heroines, obtaining the standard comic victory that Mrs. Albright does. Mrs. Monroe in *The Owl in the Attic* triumphs over the forces that befuddle her husband. Although Mother in *My Life and Hard Times* grievously misunderstands the world, she triumphs over falling beds, drunken servants, and an ineffectual husband. Mary Agnes Thurber in *The Thurber Album* repeats this vitality and shares it with Mrs. Albright. We are pleased that these women surmount their obstacles just as we are pleased to see Amy Lighter, Mrs. Mitty, or Ulgine Barrows defeated. Also in keeping with the increased power of women in the modern world, Thurber's heroines have a greater sense of their victory when it comes than do his men. Even in the bitter comedies of the 1930's, women have courage and doggedness. As the moral to one of the fables has it, "Let us ponder this basic fact about the human: Ahead of every man, not behind him, is a woman."

If Thurber is, as I have claimed, a writer who employs the structure of comedy to attain universal statement, it follows that the personages who embody his tension lack individual characteristics. The characters are identified by the vaguest and most familiar social tags: businessman, husband, teacher, editor, nurse, parent, or writer. They are, as in Greek comedy, masks expressing human drives. *The Years with Ross* therefore requires a frontispiece showing Ross; although Thurber mentions facial and body characteristics, the reader's interest is in Ross's action rather than in the accident of his appearance. Appropriately the photograph used for the frontispiece was taken by a fashionable photographer rather than by a photographer who might get behind his subject's mask. Ross looks like any successful businessman who could afford an expensive sitting. Thurber's own illustrations in the early books have the advantage of visualizing his action in abstract figures. Because these people have no blood, as Ross said, we concentrate on the comic action.

If he were not in Thurber's comic action, I doubt whether the usual Thurber hero would interest anyone. He has little occupation; whatever he does, does not challenge him. Erwin Martin in "The Catbird Seat" lives a prosaic existence at a prosaic job. Even when the man is called *Thurber*, he is more distraught than fulfilled. He is as featureless in the fiction as he is in the drawings. His adversaries likewise are simply moving men, efficiency experts, intrepid police, efficient wives, or scientists. Personality has been stripped to those qualities required for the comic struggle or tension. Thus devoid of individualizing and distracting characteristics, a single quirk such as a tendency to dream or the tip of his hat marks him sufficiently for comic interest.

The Thurber Album and *The Years with Ross* move entirely in a world of events, but Thurber's art in them is to disclose the pattern of meaning in the human experience. The essays and sketches in *Thurber Country, Lanterns and Lances,* and *Alarms and Diversions* are less flights of imagination than seemingly accurate accounts of human experience which have a natural pattern of comedy in them. I cannot prove that "A Moment with Mandy," for example, is an actual account of a colloquy between an adult and a wise child, nor that "The Porcupines in the Artichokes" is about actual difficulties that occur when one is entertaining writers at parties, but both pieces, like *Ross* and the *Album*, communicate as a mirror held up to experience, with the writer only removing spurious detail to achieve natural comedy. Thurber does not create heroes in these last books so much as he discovers them. He does not create tension; he finds struggles. The struggle, or tension, is distilled to the quintessence; it is spare, neat, essential and true to the comic vision.

The Significance of the Tension

The battle in Thurber's stories is always between a humanistic point of view and what may commonly be represented as scientism. He writes a comedy of the two cultures. Thurber's comic villains, platitudinously rationalistic in their thinking, are not true scientists. The biology instructor in "University Days" may

be a genuine scientist but Thurber presents him as a man interested only in "the mechanics of flars." Lady psychologists and
authors of popular books on dog behavior rush to judgment with
only the scantiest observation. They clamp on to experience their
own vision rather than allowing genuine truth to appear. The
clearest examples are the ineffectual palace wizards in *The White
Deer*. The King is victimized by his advisers (much as C. P. Snow
has claimed that scientists victimized politicians during the war),
and their advice only propels him more deeply into trouble rather
than extricating him. The tension between the palace wizards and
the young Prince Jorn is significant; it is the familiar story of insti-
tutional robots opposing imaginative human beings.

The mark of Thurber's insight is that he sees this struggle not
only simply but also complexly. The Thurber character who can
only see his eye in a microscope is just as much a subject for
laughter as the poor benighted instructor interested in "the mechanics of flars." While the wizards are of no particular help in
the human problems they fail to solve, they do have some function
in the kingdom, and for all of their doddering ineffectuality, they
are not banished. They have their service to perform; the only need
is to make sure that they perform the service that they can perform. Thurber castigates them as he castigates the carelessness,
mindlessness, laziness, and fragmentation that destroys the life
of the nineteenth-century men and women in *The Thurber Album*
and that opposes Ross at every weekly meeting of his editorial
staff. Thurber has the great wit to castigate his sinners without
indulging in the same sin himself; he is, therefore, much more
effective and, ultimately, more thorough than any brawling,
ranting, or raving red-eyed controversialist or idealist traducing
the virtue he would uphold. Other lady psychologists and biology
instructors may see themselves and be corrected.

Thurber's tension is significant and brave, and in its bravery
it excites a glad response. Without the bookish or the pedantic,
without parading his own *Angst* (although we know he has plenty
of it), without a single fashionable Christ symbol, Thurber advances a cause more familiar to the mouths of gentle classicists
and unread poets. He is always in his own world (and here he is
like that other American comic writer whom Thurber claimed he
read little of: Mark Twain), deriving from that world the powers

and forces of his vision. Because he is a comic writer, he advances
his cause where it can best do its good.

The Resolution

The tension of Thurber's comic drama resolves into an affir-
mative statement. Reducing it, I commit the sin against which
he complains, but I do so in expectation that Thurber's richness
is perceived along with the callowness of the reduction. The artist's
resolution is the reader's concern, for unless the resolution is clear
and pointed, the work appears aimless and formless and thus
uninteresting. It is also necessary to state Thurber's resolution
because he works in small pieces, but the small pieces have a uni-
fied point of view.

Simply stated, Thurber affirms the power of imagination.
Tommy Turner wins back his wife from the Pittsburgh steel man
because of his imagination. Erwin Martin and Walter Mitty ima-
ginatively leap ahead of their opponents. The jesters and poets
see life steadily and see it whole because they create the categories
of meaning to avert the wasteland and to bring back health. The
world is what the mind makes. Our refuge is not in the "Divine
Destiny of Man" but in the human spirit which sometimes gives
off "a magic and blinding light." In a world which appears to be
falling down, Harold Ross and Thurber's other heroes glow with
the energy and vitality of the spirit's light. The last fable in *Further Fables for Our Time* tells about the lemmings' run for the
sea and oblivion. Each lemming has some rational reason for his
run; only a scholarly old lemming remains behind and speaks what
Thurber and Prospero say:

> One male lemming who had lived alone for many years refused
> to be drawn into the stampede that swept past his cave like a
> flood. He saw no flames in the forest, and no devil, or bear, or
> goat, or ghost. He had long ago decided, since he was a serious
> scholar, that the caves of the ocean bear no gems, but only soggy
> glub and great gobs of mucky gump. And so he watched the other
> lemmings leap into the sea and disappear beneath the waves,
> some crying "We are saved!" and some crying "We are lost!"
> The scholarly lemming shook his head sorrowfully, tore up what
> he had written through the years about his species, and started
> his studies all over again.

As in "The Day the Dam Broke," human idiocy takes concrete, palpable form, and the story affirms the primacy of imaginative understanding. The moral of the fable says that "All men should strive to learn before they die what they are running from, and to, and why." Man must understand the "unbought grace" of human life rather than a reduction of life to a system or an explanation about flames, devils, bears, goats, or ghosts. The vision of Ariel is possible.

Thurber's final work accepts the human condition "without any irritable reaching after fact and reason." Although human idiocy (or sin, to speak in theological terms) runs wild, fronting idiocy with neat explanations and platitudes serves only to compound the difficulties. We live in an intractable world, but we possess genius and art to justify the experience. In the last two chapters of *The Years with Ross,* the one on Alexander Woollcott and the other on Ross himself, Ross settles into life and death more easily and humanly than Woollcott ever could. Ross, with none of Woollcott's attributes in abstract form but all of them in human form, achieved his success almost without conscious effort. Ross's triumph is a state of being that does not have to ask about values because it knows values. We are pleased by his brave stay on earth.

The Style and Texture of Thurber's World

Thurber writes, it has been said, a "styleless" style: it is so pellucid that it rarely calls attention to itself. It shows extreme care, grace, and poise but it never flaunts its qualities. Thurber's words are a clear screen through which we see his meaning, and his words support his meaning by being simple, concrete, and colloquial.

Not having distinct habits, Thurber assumes the color of other writers with ease, and thus we know he uses style consciously. His parodies, if nothing else, show his sensitivity to the angle of vision in Henry James, James Cain, and many others. The style of *Is Sex Necessary?* repeats the bumbling, inaccurate minds of the psychologists who supposedly write the book. Their startling inaccuracies communicate a judgment that statistical evidence and reasoned logic could not. In "The Psychosemanticist Will

See You Now, Mr. Thurber," Thurber suffers the disease that
the piece condemns:

> We have always been a nation of categorizationists, but what
> was once merely a national characteristic is showing signs of
> malignancy. I shall not attempt to discover the incipient primary
> lesion, for I am not a qualified research scholar in this field.
> Indeed, for having had the impudence to trespass thus far I
> shall no doubt be denounced by classificationists as a fractional
> impactionist, . . .an unauthorized incursionist, . . .a unilateral
> conclusionist, . . .and a presumptuous deductionist.

The sentences illustrate every syndrome that the essay castigates.
The style communicates as well as the denotative meaning of the
words.

The quiet, subordinated style is most typical. In an interview
published in 1955 (*Writers At Work: The Paris Review Interviews*, ed. Malcolm Cowley (New York, 1959), pp. 83-98.) Thurber explains his method. You go over and over, he says

> . . .to make the piece sound less as if you were having a lot of
> fun with it yourself. You try to play it down. In fact, if there's
> such a thing as a *New Yorker* style, that would be it—playing
> it down.

Not only does he play down the fun, he plays down the work or
trouble. Wolcott Gibb's little essay, "Theory and Practice of
Editing *New Yorker* articles," in *The Years with Ross* defines
Thurber's style in its advocacy of spareness, accuracy, gracefulness, and directness. The style is, if any such thing can be
imagined, a cautious understatement (in contrast to the bold
understatement of some British style). Thus Thurber describes
the most outrageous events in language that belies the event. "The
Night the Bed Fell"ends simply and directly:

> The situation was finally put together like a gigantic jigsaw
> puzzle. Father caught a cold from prowling around in his bare
> feet but there were no other bad results. "I'm glad," said mother,
> who always looked on the bright side of things, "that your grandfather wasn't here."

"The Night the Ghost Got In" ends with a colloquial "He had
us there." The statement is spare and complete. In *My Life and*

Hard Times accuracy is part of the joke: street names are all exact and the automobile manufacturers are correctly given. The spareness and accuracy is a function of his attitude or vision.

Thurber insists upon care, but, like the Cavalier poets who attempted careless elegance, none of the effort must show. The statement quoted above from *Writers at Work* about trying "to play it down" has little of the hallmark of Thurber's style. Statements in the same interview tell stories about Ross that are reproduced in the book on Ross, but the material in the interview is flat, pedestrian, and even midwestern. He says, for example, that Ross "was a purist and perfectionist and it had a tremendous effect on all of us: it kept us from being sloppy." The indefinite *it* and the word *tremendous* would never appear in a Thurber story except to ridicule a character who knows no better. The eight or twenty-five revisions he says each story undergoes prune out such infelicities.

Thurber uses inflection conventionally. As the book on Ross makes clear, *New Yorker* style submits itself to the discipline and tradition of the language. Gibbs advises editors to use Fowler's *A Dictionary of Modern English Usage* but not to be "precious about it." Thurber's style has restraint, appropriateness, and a purity about it that is colloquial without being common and correct without being schoolmarmish. One can give a Thurber book to a foreigner knowing that the verb tenses are accurate, that the verbs agree with their subject in number, and that the pronouns all have clear antecedents.

Gibbs advises his editors and writers to seek directness by avoiding adverbs and adjectives. Because adverbs are interdicted, Thurber's stand out, when they do appear, with the clarity of a red stripe on a white canvas. In *My Life and Hard Times,* ROTC students "moodily [creep] up on the old chemistry building." When Thurber explains to a draft board physician, "You're just a blur to me," the physician snaps back, "You're absolutely nothing to me." An exchange in *The White Deer* deliberately plays with adverbial effects. King Clode asks a woods wizard, "Have I not seen you otherwhere than here?" The sorcerer replies, "You have seen me otherwhen than now."

Thurber also attracts attention by combining an adjective from one type of sense impressions with a noun of a different category.

He once speaks of "a tall, unexpected young man." A French girl cries on "an astonished shirt." The Duke in *The Thirteen Clocks* grumbles about "chocolate chatter." Thurber speaks of the "rueful reverence" that a song like "Bye, Bye, Blackbird" deserves. His adjectives sometimes attract attention because of Thurber's tendency to alliterate the noun with its adjective (as in rueful reverence and chocolate chatter). He surprises a reader when he comments that "Ross was jocund" about an aggravation. Of all the words the reader might expect, *jocund* is not anticipated. His adjectives have a suddenness and an accuracy that delight his reader.

His nouns and verbs attempt a simple yet antic directness. He imagines that the end of the world will come "smothering, without malice or favor, gold-star mothers, collectors of internal revenue, and little laughing girls on their way to school." He likes to connect the distant and the immediate. Once, thinking of absconding, he considers whether to "fly to Zanzibar, or Mozambique, or East Liverpool, Ohio." His verbs follow the familiar textbook requirement that they be genuine action words; thus he begins the sketch about the editor who fears the declining power of middle-aged writers, "I had broken away from an undulant discussion of kinetic dimensionalism and was having a relaxed moment with a slender woman I had not seen before, who described herself as a chaoticist, when my hostess, an avid disturber of natural balances and angles of repose, dragged me off to meet the guest of honor. . . ." The *broken* and *dragged* have considerable more power than a conventional *left* and *took* which could easily substitute.

Thurber's well-constructed and well-ordered sentences sometimes have the flourish of the operatic in their balance and parallelism. During his childhood, "in the reign of Theodore Roosevelt, radio was not even a well-developed call for help at sea, much less the wondrous miracle that sends the voice of Red Skelton to the farthest corner of the earth." Lamenting his failure to write an autobiography as exciting as Salvador Dali's, he concludes, "I told too much about what went on in the house I lived in and not enough about what went on inside myself." He notes that Halley's comet will go "careening off again into the illimitable spaces upon its unfathomable rounds." Hundreds of such parallel constructions testify to his care and his wit.

He orders his sentences so that they withhold their full sense until the very end. The periodic sentence (its technical name), with its sharp thump at the end, does not appear constantly or else it would lose its effect. I find it particularly well used in the opening and closing lines of *My Life and Hard Times*. The book begins

> Benvenuto Cellini said that a man should be at least forty years old before he undertakes so fine an enterprise as that of setting down the story of his life. He said also that an auto-biographer should have accomplished something of excellence. Nowadays nobody who has a typewriter pays any attention to the old master's quaint rules.

The words are arranged in a climactic order rising to the mock climax of "quaint rules." He repeats the same technique at the end. Speaking of his desire to wander "aimlessly around the South Seas, like a character out of Conrad, silent and inscrutable" he ends, the reader will recall, by telling us that once in Martinique,

> when the whistle blew for the tourists to get back on the ship, I had a quick, wild, and lovely moment when I decided I wouldn't get back on the ship. I did, though. And I found that somebody had stolen the pants to my dinner jacket.

This final sentence keeps the reader in expectation—until we find the flat prosaic detail at the end. It may be said that Thurber is doing nothing more than following the principles of comic timing, but comic timing is a matter of word arrangement.

Comic timing is also demonstrated in his lists of words. A list may be funny because it follows the comic principle of continuing a habit or custom beyond appropriateness. A sentence from *Is Sex Necessary?* illustrates the possibility:

> By and large, love is easier to experience before it has been ex-plained—easier and cleaner. The same holds true of passion. Understanding the principles of passion is like knowing how to drive a car; once mastered, all is smoothed out; no more does one experience the feeling of perilous adventure, the misgivings, the diverting little hesitancies, the wrong turns, the false starts,

the glorious insecurity. All is smoothed out, and all, so to speak,
is lost.

The listing may also be funny because it demonstrates the sheer
vitality of the comic vision. Clearly the words are not thrown
casually on the page but are arranged with a precise sense of their
effect.

Thurber's care for the sound of his writing is apparent to anyone who has read his pieces aloud. He says they are better as
recitation pieces than they are when written down. Toward the
end of his career he complains that Americans "have never truly
loved harmony, the graceful structure of shapes and tones." No
other tongue in the world, he declares, is "as clumsy as ours is,"
but Thurber has made serious efforts to give it grace. A lemming
in a fable in *My World and Welcome to It* complains that Man is
"murderous, maladjusted, maleficent, malicious and muffle-
headed" and his history is "singularly dreary, dolorous and
distasteful." In the more straightforward essays he speaks of a
"shattered Chateau" in France and once meets a "hard and hollow
old lady." He closes a scene in "A Friend of the Earth" with a
sentence that falls into a fine and colloquial line of blank verse:

The bargain of our enmity was sealed.

It is not typical for the essays and sketches to use such regular
rhythm, but Thurber freely uses rhythm to heighten attention or
else to mark the end of a scene. Since he understates technique
and style ordinarily, his prose rhythm is unobtrusive and subdued.
When his care is noticed, his technique reinforces the reader's trust
that the writer does his work seriously.

Thurber's care is also evident in his diction and imagery. His
diction is informal, but it easily uses an occasional slang word
like *palooka* or *soup* (as "he's in the soup"). He invents words
like *strutfurrow* (a man who walks pompously in a furrow has
more pretention than he needs), and *smackwindow* (the large,
stupid insect that flies against lighted windows in early summer).
Inspired by a parlor spelling game, he invents *kissgranny, hiss-
grammer* and others. He invents new names for ship riggings. In
the fables and romances he invents *glub, gump, Golux, zish
zicker, blop, gleep, squutch, skucking, guggle* and *zatch.* And
as might be expected from a man who reads dictionaries, he uses

archaic words like *windlestraw* and *dreen.* He has some favorite words that appear often (like Shakespeare's *brave*) and acquire a Thurber meaning. He is fond of *gibbous, gibbering* and *sequelae* (rarely in the singular). The "fixed grin" marks his comic hero almost as much as his small size. Other favorite words are *chill, gloomy, irritable, jumpy, grim, perilous, murky* and all forms of the word *fear.* Because Thurber is thoroughly enchanted with the sound and shape of words, he has a true poet's devotion to them.

Ross, we are told, disliked puns, but Thurber was attracted to the forbidden fruit. He ends a piece on Henry Wallace (the 1948 Presidential candidate for the Progressive Party) speculating about Wallace supporters exclaiming, "Look Ma, I'm wallacing." He describes a firefly as a "blinking arsonist." To the report that the *New Yorker,* as analyzed by midwestern businessmen, was Red from top to bottom, Thurber replies that it wasn't even read from cover to cover. FBI investigations cause "moist qualms."

Thurber's literary allusions and use of popular writing extend the pun technique since they require a double awareness of original meaning and present application. In a fable, for example, a character is advised to be "neither a burglar nor a lender." The world, Thurber claims, is "full of sound and fury, dignifying nothing." Later, in a piece in his last book, he changes the line to say that the world is full of "sound and fury signifying nonism." Shakespeare, Henry James, Wordsworth, Coleridge, Housman, Poe, and Tennyson suffer raids from Thurber. Housman's lines,

> Loveliest of trees, the cherry now
> Is hung with bloom along the bough,
> And stands about the woodland ride
> Wearing white for Eastertide.

are transformed into,

> Loneliest of these, the married now
> Are hung with gloom along the vow,
> And stand about the wedland drear
> Dreaming dreams of yesteryear.

The skillful repetition of sound values changes this from parody into something closer to the pun. Typically the lines that Thurber

uses for these adaptations are familiar, but part of the fun in this
game is to find lines that are near enough to unknown so that we
might miss them. A good punster gets to his audience less than
fifty percent of the time; if we catch all of his puns, then the game
is unattractive. Thus Thurber twice parodies in a punning fashion
Ralph Hodgson's poem "Eve," a work surely not the common currency of *New Yorker* readers. It is not even well-known to specialists in nineteenth-century British literature. The technique
is to give the reader enough so that he recognizes the method but
to leave him also with the suspicion that if he were just a bit
brighter he would catch more. Thurber follows the same method
in "Hark the *Herald Tribune, Times,* and All the Other Angels
Sing" when he writes advertising copy for a "Super Mammoth
production in Miracolor and Vastascreen, of Wordsworth's
'Lucy.'" As with the good pun, the advertisement is so close to
being true that one could read it unsuspectingly as a genuine product of a Hollywood advertising firm. A good literary pun or a
good use of popular writing forms has the same attraction as a
metaphor, an expression that points to separate things and creates
a new awareness that could not exist before. I suspect that a
movie-going generation enjoys "The Secret Life of Walter Mitty"
because, among other reasons, the story so perfectly reflects the
tone of Hollywood war movies. We could barely sit through one
of the originals, but in Thurber's story we have the whole tone
of the original now raised to a high plane of pleasure. As with the
pun, we recognize the original meaning but enjoy the new meaning.

Occasionally Thurber's metaphors and similes stand out from
the page as if they were candidates for a file of picturesque speech.
A teacher is described as a woman "whose edges have lost their
certainty." In *The Thirteen Clocks* a ball is described as winking
and twinkling "like a naked child saluting priests." The best Thurber images have a sharp and obtrusive quality about them that
illuminates. Thurber once described himself as being oppressed
by a "grinning face. . .[that] hung over [his] house. . .like a
moon." We meet "an aged and irritable turtle." Thurber collects
his "yellow recollections and old dusty whereabouts." He juxtaposes romantic, dreamy ideas with hard observation as in the
following statement where the bravado and hyperbole of Kipling
is neatly turned aside by a second image: "I have never 'met the

tiger face to face,' as Kipling once put it, or climbed anything higher and colder than half a dozen flights of stairs." His images are social; as is appropriate for a comic writer, they come from meeting and judging people (the irritable turtle), from the events of city life (automobiles, buses, office practices), and from suburban customs. The fables and the stories for children are more free, but even in them much of the interest and charm lie in the juxtaposition of the unreal world with the world of ordinary American experience. Indeed, he is clear and flexible: he has sensed the genius of the language. He has a feeling for the value of words.

Thurber's sensitivity to language and his attempts with the pun recall the fact that he began his career with a parody (though I suspect it was a travesty) of Paul de Kruif's *Microbe Hunters.* His collaboration with E. B. White, *Is Sex Necessary?* parodies the habit of psychologists' minds, if such a thing is possible, rather than a particular psychological study. The parody of Fowler's *A Dictionary of Modern English Usage,* however, illustrates Thurber's movement into parody as a high art and into the characteristic manner and style of his age. His growth as a parodist can be illustrated by comparing a sentence from an uncollected sketch in the *New Yorker* in June, 1933, "Recollections of Henry James," with any of his later pieces. In the sketch Thurber imagines how James tells the plot of *The Bat,* a successful mystery-drama of the time, in the late Jamesian manner:

> She had been, as I have said, made, first of all to I might almost say 'feel,' as indeed so had we all, an incapacity for that way of pleasurable residence within the walls of a house for which my companion had—oh, so rightly!—the word 'contentment,' this incapacity beautifully growing out of what I shall describe as a 'warning' which the poor dear lady had 'received,' all in a by no means restrained flutter; I rather thought that the dear lady, to put, for its effect on me, a slightly more 'wingish' word, flapped—

Conrad is also present, in Thurber's imagination, at the party where James is trying to capture the essence of the personal relationship and he exclaims at this moment, "By God, there was never anything like this." Thurber is clearly writing travesty— he ridicules James by vulgarizing the Jamesian style and subjects—

rather than writing burlesque which ridicules by exaggerating style and manner. I can laugh at Thurber's version of James, but Thurber has the disadvantage of coming onto the field after Sir Max Beerbohm who burlesques James splendidly at will and who, in "The Guerdon," wrote an unsurpassed parody. Rivals bear one another loathly; Thurber never mentions Max Beerbohm despite the fact that the two share the short essay form, a skill as cartoonists, and a passionate interest in Henry James (an uncollected sketch called "The Comparable Max" is about inverting Shaw's witty epithet for Max to describe a Thurber friend). Rather than do what Max Beerbohm had done better, Thurber later attempted imitation in the way that a pun imitates. The manner of Thurber's "The Beast in the Dingle" recalls James's "The Beast in the Jungle," and the situation is Jamesian though the ending of the story is pure Thurber. As I said, Thurber takes on the Jamesian language for his own purpose. So also Thurber steals lines from Wordsworth, Browning, Eliot, or any other writer. He borrows, as well, from the movies, newspapers, or magazines (his Connecticut resembles a women's magazine version of New England). He even imitates the business letter in a sketch called "File and Forget," a series of letters to a publishing firm. The fables and the children's books are serious parodies which use the original form as another perspective just as Robert Browning uses his speakers in his dramatic monologues to give many views of experience. Thurber does what Eliot's poems, Schoenberg's music, and Picasso's paintings do when they quote older works of art. The response, in all these cases, is going to be ambiguous. Do we ridicule Eliot or Thurber as men incapable of invention for themselves when they quote Shakespeare and Wordsworth? Do we admire Picasso or Thurber for bringing back to our conscious the "Demoiselles d'Avignon" or the fable to give both a new angular style? Do we lament that a dying society proves its end when creative men prove their impotence by imitating a rich and noble past? Our pleasure may depend upon a simultaneous awareness of all three possibilities. The method that is basic to Thurber's comic view is a method that compares with that of other major writers and artists in this century and differs chiefly in the fact that Thurber writes short comic sketches usually appearing in a weekly magazine. Thurber's writing is another example of an imitative stylistic device that characterizes modern civilization in the first half of the twentieth century.

A further example of Thurber's interest in the pun and in the sound of language is his poet's ability with names. Comic writers have always played the role of Adam in naming the creatures better than the original; Aristophanes had two characters whose names may translate as Mr. Friendly Neighbor and Mr. Man-of-Good-Hope. Thurber has a penchant for names which repeat the syllabic pattern of Walter Mitty: Charlie Deshler (Deshler is the name of a Columbus hotel), Tommy Turner, Willber Kelby, and the like. He was sometimes called Jamie Thurber as a boy. Itty Bitty Walter Mitty may explain the popularity of the story since a similar story, "Mr. Pendly and the Poindexter" did not succeed nearly as well. I am most delighted by the name Mrs. Ulgine Barrows in "The Catbird Seat." Ulgine is clear enough but the Barrows is more complicated. *Barrow* is the name for a grave mound (she is dead) and it is also the name given to a castrated boar hog (she is a bore). I hope that Thurber sneaked the name by Ross. His bestiary is full of invented animals like the female Shriek and "A female Volt with all her ergs in one Casket." He shares with Henry James and Scott Fitzgerald an admirable skill in attaching names that sound right and yet are remarkably appropriate to the comic mask. His book titles deserve praise also. From *Is Sex Necessary?* (it may not be his title) to *My World and Welcome to It* and *Lanterns and Lances,* he had the poet's sharp thrust of accurate and arresting statement. The titles are, in some sense, little poems; like the sketches, they are neat, succinct, and accurate.

The texture of Thurber's language, as in the case of all fine writers, defies reduction to a neat set of principles and variations. If I could discover a simple description or explanation, then Thurber would not interest his readers; it is the variety and complication of his methods that make Thurber interesting and prevent him from becoming stale or pallid. Thurber has attracted readers because he writes well, because we recognize the texture of his vision, or whatever term describes the particular quality that his writing has. It is a comic texture or vision, and by this texture Thurber interests his reader in the bare struggle or tension. We sense the angle of his view and know that an artist has control of that slippery and elusive thing, a language, that must be subdued and ordered to create the special world that is his own. At its best, his language communicates what his words say. If we could imagine such a thing as feeling the rhythm, the texture, the images of "The First Time I Saw Paris," we would respond in the same way as we do to the statement in words, for this prose poem describes Paris in 1918 not only by its use of words but by its tone. Thurber wrote about the experience at least three times before ("The Hiding Generation" in *Let Your Mind Alone,* "An Afternoon in Paris" in *My World and Welcome to It,* and "Exhibit X" in *The Beast in Me*). By 1957 when he published a fourth version in *Holiday* magazine, he had thoroughly subdued his material to his art. The final version is a lyric response, a pure song. It is also very controlled, very understated, and very plain.

His art is considerable. It reflects the age old need of the comic writer to celebrate the human sense of jubilation in surviving. We feel the vital surge of human energy even in such despairing pieces as "The Whip-Poor-Will," "A Friend to Alexander," and "Teacher's Pet." Comic vitality ramps through *My Life and Hard Times, The Thurber Album,* and *The Years with Ross* to mark these works with the stamp of the comic vision. The comic world faces the threat of reduction, of cheap pseudo-science, and of simplification which vulgarize life to a platitude. I admire Thurber for building his comedy on the genuine tension of a society fascinated by science, psychology, and manipulation but fearful that the same powers that it admires may corrupt the meaning of society. This threat is genuinely the subject for comedy. The significant tension of our world is rescored (as a musician writes variations on a folk song or his own melody) in the two collections of fables. The method of the fables utilizes the comic technique of continuing a habit or custom (the simple and naive view of the past) in a time when the habit seems superficially inappropriate. Further, the fables use custom not just for the sake of showing us that the writer may employ an archaic form, but to speak about the human condition. The tigers, the dogs, turkeys, cats, and all his other creatures concretely recreate the forces moving in our world.

I admire particularly Thurber's own artistic and humanistic growth in his fairy tales. In these stories the implicit comic idea— that Man must triumph over sterile and unprofitable men who reduce life to a stereotype—is given explicit dramatic statement.

These stories move from a wasteland of strange, enticing, and un-usual appearance to a reality. The reality is the order made by the creative mind of the poet who reanimates the world. The world is our world, torn and dying but capable of rebirth. The American imagination has typically used the strange and distant world to project its fears, frustrations, and hopes, and thus Thurber mines a vein familiar in Hawthorne, Twain, Faulkner and Fitzgerald. Truth, beauty, and meaning exist, these stories say, not in the world nor in its social institutions, but in the mind of the Jester who discovers that the moon is just as large as the little girl who wants it imagines it to be. In truth, the moon is a golden disk caught in the branches of a tree.

Finally in two comic works, *The Thurber Album* and *The Years with Ross,* and in a spate of essays and sketches in the final decade of his life, Thurber with his new vision condemns the mid-twentieth century for its vulgarization, its unintelligence, and its blind worship of force. He praises the humanity of Harold Ross, Margery Albright, Mary Agnes Thurber, and other men and women of his childhood. In a world that is catastrophic, these men and women sense and know the true comic victory because they make their world a bright and shining place. His comedy thus praises human values and condemns what is dull and con-trary to life. It itself is a bright and shining place.

Thurber has the comic artist's need to know and discover the victory of the human spirit. Because he discovers the essence or the heart of the forces animating our world, his work is as serious and necessary as any exhaustive or statistical study of the Amer-ican condition. He has the advantage of a comic art to give his work compelling form. Thurber writes about man in society, but since the comic writer's province is society, again we must be grateful that he does so well what he set out to do, that he makes us laugh at the man menaced by a complicated civilization. Al-though his forms are small, his view is wide and intense; he sees steadily and sees whole because he has a consistent and developed point of view. Thurber is, as I started by saying, a mountain of the American imagination in the twentieth century. From his height we see ourselves and others may see us, for he is a classic of our prose and of our experience. He gives us, in balance, both Ariel and Prospero.

Works Consulted

I

I list here Thurber's publications in order of their appearance. A longer listing is found in Robert Morsberger's *James Thurber* (New York, 1964), pp. 207-18, but Morsberger wisely entitles his section "Selected Bibliography." Until an announced full bibliography appears, Morsberger is essential since he has a full list of Thurber's essays not reprinted in his books. Since I, almost exclusively, argue on the basis of Thurber's books, I include here only the titles of books. When I refer, in my text, to an essay, the book in which it appears may be discovered by checking my index.

Is Sex Necessary? Or Why You Feel the Way You Do. With
    E.B. White. New York, 1929.
The Owl in the Attic and Other Perplexities. New York, 1931.
My Life and Hard Times. New York, 1933.
The Middle-Aged Man on the Flying Trapeze. New York, 1935.
*Let Your Mind Alone, and Other More Or Less Inspirational
    Pieces.* New York, 1937.
"James Thurber," in *I Believe: The Personal Philosophies of
    Certain Eminent Men and Women in Our Time.* Ed. Clifton
    Fadiman. New York, 1939. pp. 294-300.
The Last Flower, a Parable in Pictures. New York, 1939.
Fables For Our Time and Famous Poems Illustrated. New York,
    1940.
The Male Animal. A play written in collaboration with
    Elliott Nugent. New York, 1940.
My World—and Welcome to It. New York, 1942.
Many Moons. New York, 1943.
The Great Quillow. New York, 1944.
The White Deer. New York, 1945.
The Thurber Carnival. New York, 1945. [An anthology with
    five new pieces.]
*The Beast in Me, and Other Animals, A New Collection
    of Pieces and Drawings about Human Beings and Less
    Alarming Creatures.* New York, 1948.

The 13 Clocks. New York, 1950.

The Thurber Album: A New Collection of Pieces About People. New York, 1952.

Thurber Country, A New Collection of Pieces About Males and Females, Mainly of Our Own Species. New York, 1953.

Further Fables for Our Time. New York, 1956.

The Wonderful O. New York, 1957.

Alarms and Diversions. New York, 1957. [An anthology with ten new pieces.]

The Years With Ross. Boston, 1959.

Lanterns and Lances. New York, 1961.

A Thurber Carnival (Revue). New York, 1962.

Credos and Curios. New York, 1962.

II

The following critical comments have been especially useful. Again, Morsberger's book contains a fuller list, but some of my items are not duplicated in his book.

Auden, W. H. "The Icon and the Portrait," *Nation* 150 (13 Jan 1940): 48.

Blair, Walter. *Native American Humor.* San Francisco, 1960.

_____.*Horse Sense in American Humor: From Benjamin Franklin to Ogden Nash.* Chicago, 1942.

Brady, Charles A. "What Thurber Saw," *Commonweal* 75 (8 Dec 1961): 274-76.

Breit, Harvey. *The Writer Observed.* New York, 1956.

Burke, Kenneth. "Thurber Perfects Mind Cure," *New Republic* 92 (29 Sept 1937): 220-21.

Coates, Robert M. "Thurber, Inc.," *Saturday Review* 21 (2 Dec 1939): 10-11, 28.

Cowley, Malcolm. "Lions, Lemmings, Toads and Tigers," The *Reporter* 15 (13 Dec 1956): 42-44.

_____. (ed.). *Writers at Work: The Paris Review Interviews.* New York, 1959. pp. 83-98.

DeVries, Peter. "James Thurber: The Comic Prufrock," *Poetry* 63 (1943): 150-59.

Downing, Francis. "Thurber," *Commonweal* 41 (9 Mar 1945): 518-19.

Elias, Robert E. "James Thurber: The Primitive, the Innocent, and the Individual," *American Scholar* 27 (1958): 355-63.

Ellis, James. "The Allusions in 'The Secret Life of Walter Mitty,'" *English Journal* 54 (1965): 310-13.

Friedrich, Otto. "James Thurber: A Critical Study," *Discovery* 5 (1955): 158-92.

Hackett, Francis. "Odd Man Out," *On Judging Books: In General and in Particular.* New York, 1947. pp. 29-40.

Morsberger, Robert E. *James Thurber.* Twayne's United States Authors Series, 62. New York, 1964.

Weales, Gerald. "The World in Thurber's Fables," *Commonweal* 55 (18 Jan 1957): 409-11.

Wilson, Edmund. [Review of *The White Deer*] *New Yorker* 21 (27 Oct 1945): 86-87.

III

My critical vocabulary for comedy is derived in part from the following books, but two students, Norman MacWhinney and U. J. Balducci, who have written dissertations on comedy under my direction, have taught me as much as any single book. The Enck anthology is a paperback that I have used over and over again with undergraduate classes.

Auden, W. H. *The Dyer's Hand.* New York, 1962.

Cornford, Francis. *The Origin of Attic Comedy.* New York, 1960.

Elliott, Robert G. *The Power of Satire: Magic, Ritual, Myth.* Princeton, 1960.

Enck, John J., Elizabeth T. Forter, and Alvin Whitley (eds.). *The Comic in Theory and Practice.* New York, 1960.

Feibelman, James K. *In Praise of Comedy.* New York, 1939.

Freud, Sigmund. *Wit and Its Relation to the Unconscious,* in *The Basic Writings of Sigmund Freud,* tr. A. A. Brill. New York, 1938.

Frye, Northrop. *The Anatomy of Criticism.* Princeton, 1957.

Hazlitt, William. *Lectures on the English Comic Writers.* New York, n.d.

Huizanga, J. *Homo Ludens.* New York, 1955.

Knights, L. C. "Notes on Comedy," in *The Importance of Scrutiny,* ed. Eric Bentley. New York, 1948.

Kronenberger, Louis. *The Thread of Laughter.* New York, 1952.

Langer, Susanne K. *Philosophy in a New Key.* New York, 1951.

_____. *Feeling and Form.* New York, 1953.

Orwell, George. "The Art of Donald McGill," *A Collection of Essays by George Orwell.* New York, 1954.

Potts, L. J. *Comedy.* London, 1950.

Swabey, Marie Collins. *Comic Laughter: A Philosophical Essay.* New Haven, 1961.

Sypher, Wylie. *Comedy: "Laughter" by Henri Bergson and "An Essay on Comedy" by George Meredith: "Introduction" and "Appendix: The Meanings of Comedy," by Wylie Sypher.* New York, 1956.

INDEX